World in Focus
Italy

JEN GREEN

WAYLAND

First published in 2006 by Wayland,
an imprint of Hachette Children's Books

Copyright © 2006 Wayland

All rights reserved. Apart from any use permitted under UK copyright law, this publication may only be reproduced, stored or transmitted, in any form, or by any means with prior permission in writing of the publishers or in the case of reprographic production in accordance with the terms of licences issued by the Copyright Licensing Agency.

Hachette Children's Books
338 Euston Road, London NW1 3BH

Commissioning editor: Nicola Edwards
Editor: Patience Coster
Inside design: Chris Halls, www.mindseyedesign.co.uk
Cover design: Hodder Wayland
Series concept and project management by EASI-Educational Resourcing (info@easi-er.co.uk)
Statistical research: Anna Bowden
Maps and graphs: Martin Darlison, Encompass Graphics

Printed and bound in China

British Library Cataloguing in Publication Data
Green, Jen
  Italy. - (World in focus)
  1. Italy - Juvenile literature
  I. Title
  945'.093

ISBN-10: 075024738X
ISBN-13: 978-0-7502-4738-2

NORTH TYNESIDE LIBRARIES	
014339262	
Bertrams	06.12.06
J914.5	£13.99
CYP	

Cover top: a shopping centre in Milan.
Cover bottom: a farm in Tuscany.
Title page: The main *piazza* at Amalfi near Naples.

The author and publisher would like to thank the following for allowing their pictures to be reproduced in this publication:
Corbis 5 (Massimo Mastrorillo), 10 (Rachel Royse), 11, 13 (Bettmann), 17 (Sergio Pitamitz/zefa), 22 (Enrico Oliverio/ANSA/epa), 23 (John and Lisa Merrill), 24 (Alberto Pizzoli), 25 (Alberto Pizzoli), 33 (Stephane Cardinale/People Avenue), 35 (Zohra Bensemra/Reuters), 37 (Bob Krist), 43 (Silvia Morara), 44 (Jodi Hilton), 49 (Sandro Vannini), 53 (Fabio Muzzi/Corbis Sygma), 55 (Michael S Yamashita), 59 (Peter Turnley); EASI-Images (Rob Bowden) *title page* and 21, 6, 9, 12, 16, 19, 20, 28, 29, 30, 31, 32, 34, 36, 39, 41, 45, 46, 50, 54, 56; EASI-Images (Ed Parker) 14, 15, 18, 26, 27, 38, 40, 48, 51, 52, 57, 58; Chris Fairclough Worldwide/Chris Fairclough 4, 8, 42, 47.

The website addresses (URLs) included in this book were valid at the time of going to press. However, because of the nature of the Internet, it is possible that some addresses may have changed, or sites may have changed or closed down since publication. While the author and publishers regret any inconvenience this may cause the readers, no responsibility for any such changes can be accepted by either the author or the publisher.

The directional arrow portrayed on the map on page 7 provides only an approximation of north.

The data used to produce the graphics and data panels in this title were the latest available at the time of production.

CONTENTS

1	Italy – An Overview	4
2	History	8
3	Landscape and Climate	14
4	Population and Settlements	18
5	Government and Politics	22
6	Energy and Resources	26
7	Economy and Income	30
8	Global Connections	34
9	Transport and Communications	38
10	Education and Health	42
11	Culture and Religion	46
12	Leisure and Tourism	50
13	Environment and Conservation	54
14	Future Challenges	58
	Timeline	60
	Glossary	61
	Further Information	62
	Index	63
	About the Author	64

CHAPTER 1

Italy – An Overview

With an outline that is instantly recognizable, the country of Italy is made up mainly of a slender, boot-shaped peninsula jutting into the northern Mediterranean, along with two large islands, Sicily and Sardinia. To the north, Italy shares borders with France, Switzerland, Austria and Slovenia. Italy is about the same size as the US state of Arizona. It has a highly successful economy and in 2005 was ranked as the seventh wealthiest economy in the world. Italy's economic strength is partly a result of its strategic position at the centre of Europe. As a member of the European Union (EU), Italy has an economy linked with other EU members, such as France and Germany. In 2002, Italy's adoption of the single European currency (the Euro) led to still closer ties with other EU members that had also adopted the Euro.

OLD AND NEW

Italy is both an ancient country and a fairly young one. Italian culture has influenced the Mediterranean region for many hundreds of years, yet 150 years ago the unified country called Italy did not exist. Two thousand years ago, Italy was home to one of the ancient world's most advanced civilizations, the Roman Empire. Around AD 100, the Romans ruled a vast empire that included many of the lands bordering the Mediterranean Sea.

After the fall of the Roman Empire in the fifth century, Italy was divided into a series of small

▼ Italy's capital, Rome, includes the Vatican City within its borders. St Peter's Square, shown here, is the heart of the Vatican.

city-states (see page 10), often ruled by foreign powers. However, the influence of Italian culture remained strong in Europe and beyond. As the home of the papacy, the city of Rome became the centre of western Christianity. Throughout medieval times, the popes wielded great worldly, as well as spiritual, power (see pages 48-9). During the fourteenth to sixteenth centuries, the region of Italy found itself at the heart of a great artistic awakening known as the Renaissance. Italian painters, sculptors, poets and other artists produced great art treasures and writings (see page 46).

UNIFICATION

In the 1850s, the movement to unify Italy gathered pace. In 1861, the various political regions were brought together as a single country. During the twentieth century, Italy met with mixed fortunes. It sided with Germany during the Second World War and suffered a disastrous defeat. During the 1950s, Italy industrialized rapidly and its economy boomed, though economic progress later slowed.

As citizens of a leading industrial nation, most Italians enjoy a fairly high standard of living. However, a deep divide exists between northern and southern Italy in terms of living standards and resources. The north is wealthy and more industrialized, while the south is poorer and more agricultural. Since the 1950s, successive Italian governments have tried to lessen this divide by spending large sums of money on improving the resources and industries of the south, but with varying degrees of success. In the north, the 1990s saw the rise of political parties campaigning for the region to cut its ties with the south, and become more independent. This campaign gained considerable support among people in the north.

Did you know?

Two small, independent countries are located inside Italy's borders: the tiny republic of San Marino dating back to AD 301, and the Vatican City inside Rome.

◀ Renaissance Italy produced a wealth of great art treasures. A copy of Michelangelo's sculptural masterpiece, *David*, can be seen standing outside the Palazzo Vecchio in Florence. The original statue is situated inside the Galleria dell'Accademia, also in Florence.

PEOPLE AND LANGUAGE

Around 96 per cent of Italy's people are ethnic Italians (including Sardinians, who view the large island of Sardinia as partly separate from mainland Italy). Small numbers of French, Germans and Slovenes live near Italy's northern borders, with Albanians and Greeks in the south of the country. Italian is a 'Romance' language, derived from Latin and based on a dialect spoken in Tuscany in medieval times. Around the year 1900, only a few of Italy's people spoke what is now standard Italian, the rest spoke regional dialects. Today, dialects are used mainly just by the older generation. Italy's long history as a group of city-states has left Italians with a sense of regional identity which can appear stronger than their sense of national identity. Many people see themselves firstly as belonging to a particular city or region, and secondly as Italian.

ITALY'S REPUTATION

Italy's historic cities, rich culture and sunny climate are world renowned. They attract holidaymakers, and tourism is central to Italy's economy. Italy is also famed as the land of fast cars, high fashion, opera and romance. The national flair for design ensures that Italian clothes, cars and other products sell well abroad. The country is also famous for its cuisine (cooking). Italian-style foods such as pizza, pasta and ice-cream are eaten all over the world.

Italy is also well known for some less positive aspects of its culture. It is notorious as a base for organized crime – especially that of the international criminal organization known as the Mafia, which is involved in the illegal drugs trade. Since the 1990s, Italy has been rocked by a series of scandals, with accusations of bribery, corruption and even violence being levelled at leading politicians and businessmen. Such accusations are still being made today.

Physical geography

- Land area: 294,020 sq km/113,521 sq miles
- Water area: 7,210 sq km/2,784 sq miles
- Total area: 301,230 sq km/116,305 sq miles
- World rank (by area): 70
- Land boundaries: 1,932 km/1,200 miles
- Border countries: Austria, France, Holy See (Vatican City), San Marino, Slovenia, Switzerland
- Coastline: 7,600 km/4,723 miles
- Highest point: Monte Bianco de Courmayeur, secondary peak of Mont Blanc (4,748 m/ 15,577 ft)
- Lowest point: Mediterranean Sea (0 m/0 ft)

NB: all the above data includes Sardinia and Sicily

Source: CIA World Factbook

◀ The Italian diet includes plenty of fresh produce, much of which is grown locally. This stall is selling fresh citrus juices.

Italy – An Overview 7

CHAPTER 2

History

The first settlements in Italy grew up around 4,000 BC, although evidence of human remains have been found dating from 20,000 BC. During the ninth century BC, Phoenicians from the North African city of Carthage colonized southern Italy. Later on, invaders from Greece arrived and claimed much of Italy as part of the Greek Empire. By the seventh century BC, a people called the Etruscans had dominated central Italy and formed an association of twelve city-states, called Etruria.

▼ Public entertainments were staged in amphitheatres like this throughout the Roman world. Gladiator contests, and even re-enactments of sea battles, were staged here at the Colosseum in Rome.

THE ROMAN EMPIRE

According to legend, Rome was founded in 753 BC. In 509 BC, a Latin-speaking people, the Latini, who probably originated north of the Alps, drove the Etruscan king out of Rome and founded the Roman republic. Through a series of wars, the Romans carved out an empire which, by AD 100, stretched from Britain east to Syria, and south into North Africa. The Romans were skilled architects and engineers, and built a network of roads, forts and towns throughout their empire. They constructed aqueducts to carry water, and introduced new farming practices and other innovations that made life easier. Wealthy Romans lived comfortably in town houses or country villas

complete with central heating and sanitation. In large estates and well-to-do households, slaves did much of the work.

Jesus Christ lived and died in the Roman province of Palestine in the Middle East. During the early centuries AD, Christianity took hold in the Roman world, replacing other religions. At first the new religion was outlawed, but in AD 313 the Roman emperor, Constantine, allowed Christians to worship. Rome soon became the base of the papacy (see page 48). In the third century, the Roman Empire was divided in half to make it easier to administrate. The western half was ruled from Rome, the eastern half from Byzantium (later called Constantinople, now Istanbul in Turkey). The Western Empire came under increasing threat from warlike peoples to the north, whom the Romans called Barbarians. In AD 476, the Barbarian leader Odoacer sacked Rome and deposed the last emperor. In the east, the Byzantine Empire remained strong.

 Did you know?

The Romans were responsible for Italy's name. They called the southern part of the country *Italia*, which means 'land where oxen graze'.

Focus on: Vesuvius and Pompeii

In AD 79, the volcano known as Mount Vesuvius near the city of Naples erupted without warning. From a nearby vantage point, the Roman writer Pliny the Younger saw a great cloud of dark ash rise from the mountain and spread across the sky. The cloud of burning ash engulfed the town of Pompeii at the foot of Vesuvius, and all the inhabitants perished. In the eighteenth century, Pompeii was rediscovered and excavated. The thick layer of ash had preserved the town's streets perfectly. Elaborate mosaics and frescos were found intact in wealthy villas. The imprints of the bodies of Pompeii's citizens and even their pets had also been preserved by the ash.

◀ The Roman town of Pompeii is now a major tourist attraction. Streets, buildings and even graffiti on walls have been preserved by the volcanic ash which fell on the town almost two thousand years ago.

Following the breakup of the Western Empire, the geographical region of Italy was divided into a number of smaller territories, many of which became parts of other empires. Meanwhile the popes grew more powerful, and acquired much of central Italy, which became known as the Papal States. Between the ninth and fourteenth centuries, successive popes vied for control of northern Italy. To the north, the Holy Roman Empire ruled much of western Europe. To the south, Byzantium ruled southern Italy and was later succeeded by the Arabs, the Normans and the Spanish.

CITY-STATES AND FOREIGN RULE

The tenth to fourteenth centuries saw the rise of small, independent city-states across much of Italy. Each of these states was centred on a city such as Venice, Genoa, Milan, Florence or Pisa, and governed either by a council of elders or a wealthy merchant or nobleman. City-states such as Milan, Genoa and Venice grew prosperous through trade and banking, and Venice even established an empire of its own. The rulers of Italian city-states were important patrons of the arts, who supported the great artistic flowering of the Renaissance.

Between 1500 and 1800, much of Italy was ruled by foreign powers such as France, Spain and Austria. Following the French Revolution in 1789-92, the French emperor, Napoleon Bonaparte, conquered northern Italy and set up a series of

▼ The Norman rulers of Sicily were great builders, and their architectural influence can be seen in the sweeping lines of this cathedral in Palermo. The Normans employed Arabic craftsmen to decorate the interiors with dazzling mosaics.

History 11

republics. After Napoleon's defeat in 1815, Italy was returned to its former state, with the north ruled by Austrians, the south by the Spanish, and the centre by the Papal States. But Napoleon's occupation of Italy had given many of its people a taste for a unified, independent nation. The independent kingdom of Piedmont and the island of Sardinia became a focus for unification.

Did you know?

Around AD 1300, approximately four hundred separate city-states flourished in Italy.

▼ A fifteenth-century woodcut of the port of Genoa. This city-state, a leading centre for trade, was the birthplace of Christopher Columbus.

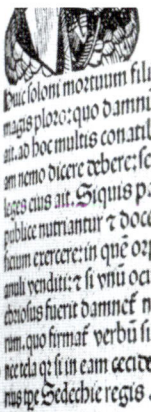

Focus on: Italian explorers

In medieval times, many great travellers and explorers came from Italy. In the late thirteenth century, a young Venetian, Marco Polo, was one of the first Europeans to visit China. He wrote a famous book about his travels. In 1492, Christopher Columbus, a navigator from Genoa, was commissioned by the Spanish to sail across the Atlantic. His mission was to reach China and the east, but he discovered the 'New World' of the Americas instead. Another Italian explorer, Amerigo Vespucci, gave his name to the Americas. In the fifteenth century, the Venetian navigator Giovanni Caboto, known as John Cabot, explored the coast of Canada.

UNIFICATION AND WORLD WAR

In the 1850s, the *Risorgimento*, or movement to unify the diverse states of Italy, gathered strength. Unification was achieved through three key figures: Giuseppe Mazzini, a political activist, Count Camillo Cavour, chief minister of Piedmont-Sardinia, and Giuseppe Garibaldi, a brilliant soldier. In 1859, Cavour's forces defeated the Austrians in northern Italy.

The army of Piedmont moved south, while Garibaldi invaded Sicily with a force of 1,000 men and swept north. The independent Kingdom of Italy, proclaimed in 1861, was soon enlarged by the addition of Venice and the Papal States.

From the late 1800s, Italy took part in the 'scramble for Africa', when European powers competed to seize African territories. Italy took control of Eritrea, Somalia and Libya. During the First World War, Italy sided with the Allies in an attempt to increase its territory, but did not make substantial gains. In the 1920s, the fascist leader Benito Mussolini rose to power by promising to make Italy a great nation. In 1922, the fascists marched on Rome and the king, Victor Emmanuel III, declared Mussolini as premier of Italy. By 1925, Mussolini had become a dictator, with absolute authority.

In 1936, Italian forces occupied Ethiopia in East Africa. In 1940, Italy entered the Second World War on the side of Nazi Germany, but was defeated by the Allies, who by 1943 had occupied southern Italy. The Italian government surrendered and overthrew Mussolini, but the Nazis took control and installed Mussolini as head of a puppet state in the north. Italy became a war zone, as Allied forces and Italian partisans (resistance fighters opposed to the Nazis) battled their way north up the country. By 1945, Mussolini had been killed and the Allies were victorious.

◀ A statue of Italian national hero Giuseppe Garibaldi. His force of 1,000 volunteers were nicknamed 'redshirts'. In 1860 they conquered Sicily and then Naples.

INTO THE TWENTY-FIRST CENTURY

After the war, much of Italy lay in ruins. However, with the help of the USA, the post-war period brought rapid economic growth and industrialization. In 1957, Italy became a founding member of the European Economic Community (EEC). But in the 1960s Italy's economy slowed and inflation rose (see page 30).

The 1970s brought turmoil, with the rise of right-wing and left-wing terrorist groups opposed to all political parties. Some of these groups carried out bombings, kidnappings and murders. In 1978, a left-wing extremist group called the Red Brigades kidnapped and killed a former prime minister, Aldo Moro. The mid-1980s brought better times, with partial economic recovery and the defeat of terrorism. However, during the 1990s the Italian government was involved in a series of political scandals, with many politicians accused of criminal activities. Italy's attempts to stamp out organized crime and corruption have continued into the twenty-first century (see pages 24-5).

▼ Benito Mussolini (left) and Nazi leader Adolf Hitler watch a parade held when the Italian dictator visited Germany in 1937.

CHAPTER 3

Landscape and Climate

With a land area of 294,020 sq km (113,521 sq miles), Italy is smaller than France, but larger than the United Kingdom. The boot-shaped peninsula of Italy is nowhere more than 170 km (105 miles) wide, but it is 1,200 km (745 miles) long. Italy is surrounded by the seas of the Mediterranean on three sides: the Ligurian Sea to the north-west, the Adriatic to the east, the Tyrrhenian Sea to the west and the Ionian Sea to the south-east.

Italy's coastline stretches 7,600 km (4,723 miles). The 'toe' of Italy lies close to the island of Sicily, the Mediterranean's largest island which covers 25,709 sq km (9,926 sq miles). The rocky island of Sardinia, occupying 24,089 sq km (9,300 sq miles), lies to the west across the Tyrrhenian Sea. In addition, Italy has more than 3,000 smaller islands, such as Elba and Capri.

MOUNTAINS AND LOWLANDS

Much of Italy is covered by uplands. In the far north, the Alps are Italy's highest mountains, rising to 4,748 m (15,577 ft) on the slopes of Mont Blanc, whose summit is in France. The Alps form the national border with France, Switzerland and Austria. East of the Alps rise the Dolomites, a range of craggy limestone peaks. The Apennines form a rugged mountain crest zigzagging down central Italy for some 1,350 km (840 miles).

Lowlands cover less than a quarter of Italy. A large lowland belt lies in the north, sandwiched between the Alps and the

▼ Snow lingers in the Italian Alps late into summer. However, the region's glaciers are shrinking because of global warming.

Landscape and Climate   15

Apennines. Here the plain of Lombardy in the west merges with the Po valley to the east. This region is extensively farmed and densely populated. Other low-lying plains are found along parts of the west coast and in Puglia, which forms Italy's 'heel'.

Italy's longest river is the Po, which rises in the Alps and flows 652 km (405 miles) to the Adriatic. Other rivers include the Adige, the Tiber and the Arno. In the south, some rivers (called *fiumare*) dry up in summer. The large, beautiful lakes of Garda, Maggiore and Como are in the north, with Lake Trasimeno in central Italy.

Italy lies on a geological fault line, a zone of weakness in the earth's crust. Magma (molten rock) surging up through cracks (faults) in the earth's crust produces volcanic eruptions. Italy's volcanoes include Mount Etna on Sicily and the volcanic island of Stromboli. Mount Vesuvius, near Naples, famously erupted in AD 79 (see page 9), and more recently in 1631 and 1944. Some experts believe another eruption of Vesuvius is due.

 Did you know?
The word 'volcano' comes from the small volcanic island of Vulcano off the coast of southern Italy.

◄ There are frequent minor eruptions from the crater on Mount Stromboli, on one of the Aeolian islands off the coast of Sicily. Red-hot rocks shoot into the air and fall into the sea with a hissing sound.

Focus on: Where plates collide

Italy is located on a border zone where two of the huge tectonic plates that form the earth's crust meet and push together. Millions of years ago, these same plates, the European and African plates, created the Alps, fold mountains which formed as rock crumpled upwards as the plates collided. The enormous pressure created by the plate collision also causes rocks to shift, sometimes producing violent earthquakes. Central and southern Italy are particularly prone to earthquakes. The last major earthquake was in 2002 and measured 5.9 on the Richter scale.

CLIMATE

Italy is renowned for its sunny climate, and its skies are mostly clear during spring, summer and autumn. In winter, the skies are often overcast and rainy. In spring, hot, dry air from Africa moves north to cover much of Italy. Summers (June-August) are mainly dry, with occasional thunderstorms. In autumn, cool, moist air moves in from the Atlantic Ocean. Winter (December-February) brings the coolest temperatures.

The height of the land and its closeness to the sea affect local climates, and result in cooler uplands and some milder climates near the coast. Italy's long north-south extent also brings regional variations in climate, which are most obvious in winter. Much of the north has a temperate climate, meaning it is cooler and

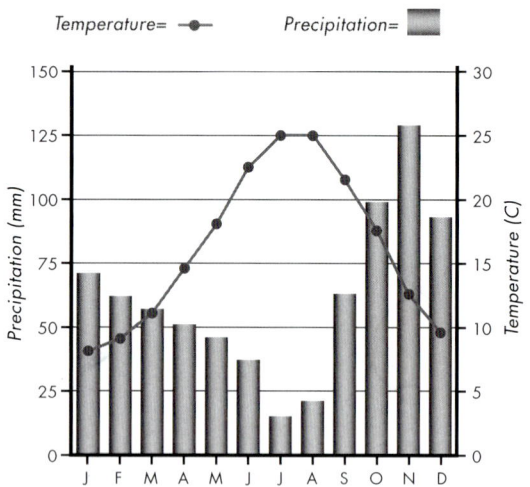

▲ Average monthly climate conditions in Rome

▼ The dry climate means that much of southern Italy is covered by scrubby vegetation. This is the coast around the town of Vietri sul Mare, south of Naples.

Landscape and Climate

wetter than southern areas. The city of Milan experiences average minimum temperatures of 1°C (35°F) in January, while temperatures climb to 28°C (82°F) in summer. Italy's climate becomes progressively hotter and drier further south. Palermo in Sicily has an average January minimum of 8°C (44°F), with temperatures soaring to 30°C (86°F) in summer. Southern Italy is known as the *Mezzogiorno* – the land of the midday sun – because of the scorching heat around noon in summer. Parts of the south and centre are extremely dry, and gripped by drought from time to time.

VEGETATION

Regional differences in climate and terrain suit different types of vegetation, giving rise to a variety of scenery. In the north, the lower slopes of the Alps are clothed in forests of fir and pine, with alpine meadows higher up. Forests of oak, beech and pine once covered much of Italy, but these were mostly felled long ago for timber and agriculture. Farming has totally transformed lowland areas like the Po valley, while coastal marshlands have been drained for agriculture. Cypress trees dot the rolling hills of Tuscany in the west. Dense, thorny scrubland called *macchia* covers dry, stony terrain in the south and on Sardinia.

Focus on: Natural disasters

With earthquakes, volcanic eruptions, droughts and floods, Italy has its fair share of natural disasters. In 1908, the port of Messina in Sicily was devastated by a violent earthquake that killed more than 70,000 people. Mount Etna on Sicily is one of Europe's highest active volcanic mountains. Major eruptions occurred here in 1996 and in 2002. In 1994, torrential rains in north-west Italy caused extensive flooding, in which about one hundred people died.

Did you know?

The climate of southern and central Italy – hot, dry summers and mild winters – is known as a Mediterranean climate, wherever it occurs worldwide.

▼ Tall cypress trees frame a farm on a hilltop in Tuscany, providing protection from chill winter winds.

CHAPTER 4

Population and Settlements

In 2005, there were just over 57 million people living in Italy. Between 1850 and 1970, Italy's population rose steeply, but since 1995, the figure has remained almost constant. In the 1950s, the population increased by about 7 per cent each year, but growth fell to less than 4 per cent in the 1980s, and to zero by the mid-1990s. This so-called zero population growth occurs when numbers of births and deaths are equal, and therefore cancel each other out.

By 2005, Italy's population had actually started to fall slightly. Experts predict that this trend will continue over the next decades (see graph). From having a population equal in size to that of France and the UK, Italy's looks set to fall to a similar level to that of Spain today. On average, Italian families have only 1.2 children – fewer than the average of 2.05 children needed to keep the population the same size. There are many reasons for this, including the fact that Italians are marrying later, and that more women are going out to work before and after marriage. Many families want a lifestyle they could not afford if they had more children. In general, family sizes are larger in the south than in the north.

In 2003, just over two-thirds of the population were aged between 15 and 64, with only 14 per cent under the age of 15. Almost one-fifth of Italians were aged 65 and over, with better healthcare helping people to live longer. This pattern is similar in many European countries. The government fears that, in twenty years' time, not enough adults will be working and paying taxes to support the large numbers of older people who need pensions, increased medical care and other services. Italy's government is now encouraging people to work longer and retire later.

◄ High-rise housing is found in suburbs and in the centres of Italian cities. Modern apartment blocks are a common feature. The apartments shown here were built during the 1960s in a suburban area of Rome.

Population and Settlements   19

NORTH AND SOUTH

In 2004, Italy had an average population density of about 190 people per sq km (492 per sq mile). However, the population is not evenly distributed. More people live in fertile lowlands and industrial areas, while mountains and dry areas have fewer people. In the nineteenth and twentieth centuries, a marked contrast developed between northern and southern Italy in terms of population and industrial development. The north became more densely populated, with a climate and terrain favourable for farming, more natural resources and better developed industries. Fewer people lived in the south, with its harsh climate, poor farms and less developed industries.

▲ Men enjoy a game of cards at a social club in Sorrento. The proportion of the population aged 65 and over is steadily increasing.

 Did you know?

Many Italians live in *palazzos*. A *palazzo* is not a palace, as the Italian word implies, but an apartment block.

Population data

- Population: 57.3 million
- Population 0-14 yrs: 14%
- Population 15-64 yrs: 67%
- Population 65+ yrs: 19%
- Population growth rate: -0.1%
- Population density: 190.2 per sq km/492.7 per sq mile
- Urban population: 67%
- Major cities: Milan 4,007,000
  Naples 2,905,000
  Rome 2,628,000

Source: United Nations and World Bank

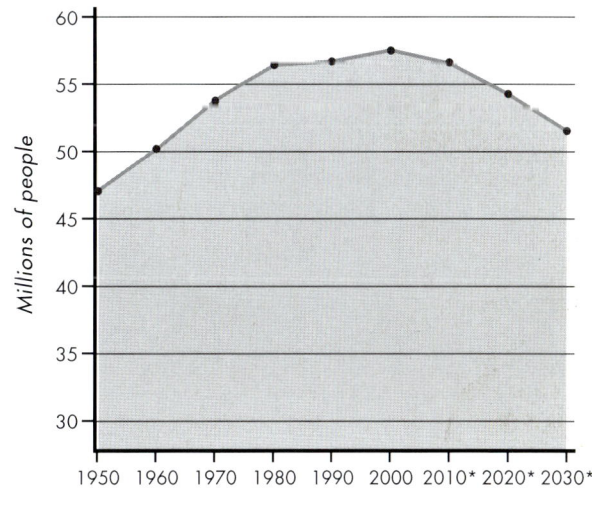

* Projected Population

▲ Population growth, 1950-2030

In the 1950s and 1960s, large numbers of Italians from the south moved to the industrial centres of the north to seek work and a better standard of living. This caused problems such as unemployment and overcrowding in some northern cities, while some villages in the south became deserted. Between 1950 and 1984, the Italian government spent huge sums on the *Cassa per il Mezzogiorno*, a fund to develop the industries, communications and resources of the south. The fund succeeded in areas such as the improvement of transport, but efforts to relocate industry and business met with mixed results. The south still lags behind the north in natural resources, and its climate is less favourable to farming.

ITALIAN CITIES

Just over two-thirds of Italy's population live in urban areas, a figure that has remained roughly constant since 1995. This urban figure is low compared with that of many European countries. From ancient times, settlements grew up in Italy in favoured sites, such as cool hilltops and fertile river valleys, that offered water for irrigation, a means of transport and defence against enemies. Unlike most other countries, Italy is not dominated by a single city. Milan, Rome and Naples are the three largest cities, with over 2.5 million people each. Turin, Bari, Bologna, Florence, Genoa, Catania, Palermo and Venice are also major conurbations. Each has a distinct character, dating from the days of the city-states. For example, in medieval times, the city of Venice grew wealthy through trade and carved out an empire based on naval supremacy.

◀ The scene in this narrow backstreet in Naples is typical of many cities in southern Italy.

Population and Settlements 21

Italian towns are traditionally laid out around one or more squares (*piazze*). Many towns have fine buildings, including churches, dating back to Renaissance, medieval and even Roman times. Older districts have large, handsome houses built around a central courtyard. In modern suburbs, many people live in apartments in high-rise buildings. The poorest housing is often on the outskirts of towns and cities. Although they have great historic interest, Italian cities are not exempt from problems that plague urban areas the world over, including traffic congestion, overcrowding in poor districts, and pollution.

▶ Every Italian town has at least one *piazza*, although not all are as grand as this one in Amalfi, near Naples.

Focus on: Rome

Rome, 'the eternal city', is Italy's capital and second largest city, after Milan. Its many historic buildings include the Forum, where Romans worshipped and did business, and the Colosseum, where gladiatorial contests were staged. Originally built around seven hills at a crossing on the River Tiber, the city is also known for the underground catacombs where early Christians buried their dead. It is the only city in the world with an independent country inside it – the Vatican. Rome is renowned for its graceful squares and fountains dating from around 1600. In the twentieth century, Rome grew rapidly with the construction of many high-rise offices and apartment blocks. Rome became a thriving centre for finance, trade and industry, including the fashion industry. Modern Rome is a mixture of grand old buildings and modern blocks, with crowded cafés, brightly-lit stores, and noisy traffic winding its way through narrow backstreets.

CHAPTER 5

Government and Politics

In 1946, Italians voted to abolish their country's monarchy and Italy has been a republic ever since. In 1947, the nation's constitution was written to prevent the rise of another dictator like Mussolini. Italy is a parliamentary democracy. Everyone over the age of 18 has the right to vote. The percentage of the population that votes in elections is high compared with many countries. Referendums are sometimes held on major issues such as abortion and electoral reform.

Italy is divided into 20 administrative regions, each of which has a strong identity. All regions have a degree of self-rule and a few, including Sardinia, have considerable autonomy (independence). The regions are subdivided into provinces, and the provinces are divided into units called communes.

ELECTORAL SYSTEM

Italy's parliament, based in Rome, is made up of two houses. Italy's electoral system was reformed in 1993. Seventy-five per cent of members of both houses are directly elected, with the candidate with the most votes in an area winning the seat, and the other parties winning nothing. The remaining 25 per cent of members are elected through the system of proportional representation. With this system, seats are given to parties according to their share of the vote in the whole country. The upper house, or Senate, has 315 members, 232 of whom are directly elected and 83 of whom are elected from the regions by proportional representation. The lower house, the Chamber of Deputies, has 630 members, 475 of whom are directly elected and 155 of whom are elected through the system of proportional representation. Senators and deputies serve a five-year term. There are relatively few women in parliament compared with some European countries.

Did you know?

Voting is considered a 'civic duty' in Italy. Failure to vote in elections is an offence and can lead to a criminal record.

◀ Pope John Paul II addresses the Chamber of Deputies in 2002. Pope John Paul died in 2005, and was succeeded by Pope Benedict XVI.

The president occupies the largely ceremonial position of head of state. However, in recent years presidents have taken an active role during times of political turmoil, for example, during the *Tangentopoli* scandal (see page 24). Presidents serve a seven-year term. The prime minister, the leader of the most powerful party in government, chooses the cabinet of ministers. Prime ministers do not serve a fixed term and Italy is famous for its frequent changes of prime minister and cabinet. However, many ministers continue to serve in the governments of successive prime ministers, which provides continuity.

▼ The seat of local government – the town hall and main square of Cortona in Tuscany.

POST-WAR POLITICS

Since the Second World War, Italy's complex electoral system has resulted in governments being formed through coalitions, meaning that a number of political parties has shared power. From 1948 to the mid-1990s, the centre-right Christian Democrat Party, with a broadly conservative outlook, dominated Italian politics. The Christian Democrats formed coalitions with other parties, including socialists and liberals, but kept the Communist Party out of government, despite the fact that it had considerable support.

 Did you know?

Since the Second World War, few Italian governments have lasted much more than a year.

Since the 1950s, successive governments have steered Italy's economy while trying to tackle persistent problems, including inflation, unemployment and organized crime in the form of the Mafia (see box opposite). The north-south divide has remained a difficult and lasting issue. During the 1990s, a political party called the *Lega Lombardia* (Northern League) gained considerable support in the north. The League wants the north to become more independent, or even a separate country, and to stop subsidizing the south.

CORRUPTION CHARGES

The early 1990s witnessed a political crisis that changed the face of Italian politics. In 1992, investigations into party finances uncovered a web of bribery and corruption that reached the highest levels of government. Leading businessmen and politicians from every major party were accused of criminal dealings and links with the Mafia. The best known of these was Giulio Andreotti, a leading Christian Democrat who had been prime minister six times. The scandals were called *Tangentopoli* (*tangente* means bribe and *poli* city in Italian).

Following these scandals, the public lost confidence in existing political parties, and new political alliances were formed. In 1994, the election was won by the centre-right Alliance for Freedom, which included the *Forza Italia* (Come on, Italy) Party, led by Silvio Berlusconi, head of the media empire Fininvest. However, Berlusconi was soon forced to resign following accusations of corruption. His departure enabled the centre-left Olive Tree Alliance to take power in the late 1990s. Despite this, Berlusconi was re-elected in 2001. The general election of April 2006 resulted in victory for the centre-left party, the Union, led by Romano Prodi, who replaced Berlusconi.

▼ Former prime minister Giulio Andreotti (centre), was implicated in the *Tangentopoli* scandals of 1992-3. He is seen here after being tried and acquitted on the charge that he protected the Mafia while he was prime minister.

Focus on: The Mafia

The Mafia is a criminal organization with links worldwide, including in the USA. It dates back to medieval times in Sicily, where it grew as a secret organization whose aim was to overthrow foreign rule. Members of the Mafia (*mafiosi*) are bound by a code of silence (*omertà*), which forbids them to betray other *mafiosi*, even rival groups, to the police. By the early twentieth century, the Mafia controlled much of southern Italy. Mussolini almost broke the Mafia's power by imprisoning many of its leaders, but the organization regained strength following the Second World War, when it became increasingly involved in the illegal drugs trade.

Over the years, Mafia members have carried out the assassinations of police officers and judges: killings include those of the Sicilian anti-Mafia judge Giovanni Falcone and his colleague Paolo Borsellino in 1992. In Italy, the Mafia is known as *la piovra*, the octopus, because its tentacles reach everywhere. Nevertheless, public disgust at Mafia killings and threats has been demonstrated more openly in recent times. Since the 1990s, the police have also scored notable successes in arresting a number of Mafia leaders, including Salvatore Riina (arrested in 1993), Leoluca Bagarella (1995), Giovanni Brusca (1996), Vito Vitale (1998) and Mariano Trioa (2006).

▲ In May 1992, a large crowd attends the funeral of murdered judge Giovanni Falcone in Palermo, Sicily, to show support for his anti-Mafia stance.

CHAPTER 6

Energy and Resources

Italy's natural resources include minerals, forests, farmland, and fish in the surrounding waters. However, resources for energy are fairly scarce, and this has restricted the growth of industry and profits from manufacturing.

ENERGY RESOURCES AND USE

Italy has limited reserves of fossil fuels, including oil, natural gas and lignite coal. Oil and natural gas are pumped in the Po valley, Calabria, Sicily, and offshore in the south. Nuclear power provides a relatively small amount of the country's energy. This form of energy is mainly undeveloped following a 1987 referendum in which Italians voted overwhelming against the construction of more nuclear plants. Public opposition to nuclear power deepened following an accident in 1986 at the Chernobyl nuclear reactor in Ukraine. In terms of renewable energy sources, Italy's hydro-electric (HEP) potential is well developed. Hydro-electric plants in the Alps and the Apennines harness the energy of fast-flowing streams to provide power for cities and industry. One of the world's first geothermal plants was built at Larderello. Here, cold water pumped underground is heated by volcanic rocks and used to produce steam, which drives turbines to generate electricity. Use of solar power is limited at present but, with Italy's sunny climate, this form of energy has considerable potential. Italy has one of the fastest growing wind sectors in the world, and wind and wave power could be utilized more extensively in future.

In 1999, Italy consumed 1.7 per cent of all the energy used worldwide. Nearly one-third of this was used in transport, with homes consuming around another quarter and industry a third. Italy's limited energy sources do not meet its power needs. Some 75 per cent of the energy it uses is imported, mostly in the form of oil and natural gas. The nation's power plants burn mainly oil imported from Libya, Iran and other oil-producing nations.

◀ In mountainous parts of Italy, hydro-electric plants are used to generate electricity. Around 17 per cent of Italy's electricity is produced by HEP.

Energy and Resources

Energy data

- Energy consumption as % of world total: 1.7%
- Energy consumption by sector (% of total),
  Industry: 31.7
  Transportation: 32.2
  Agriculture: 2.4
  Services: 3.5
  Residential: 26.9
  Other: 3.3
- CO_2 emissions as % of world total: 1.8
- CO_2 emissions per capita in tonnes p.a.: 7.3

Source: World Resources Institute

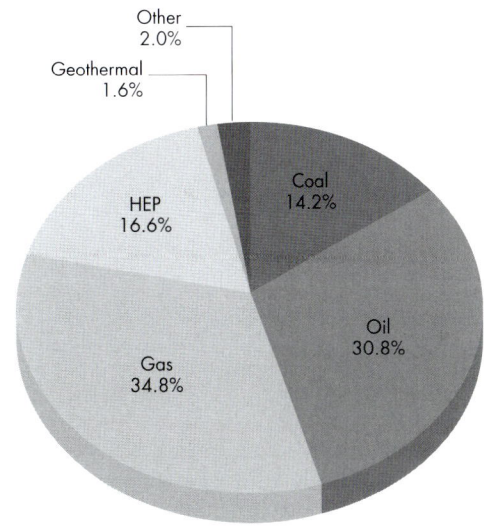

▲ Electricity production by type

Focus on: Carrara marble

The town of Carrara in the Apennines in Tuscany produces top quality marble for use in construction and sculpture. Mining began here in Roman times. Marble, a hard, attractively veined rock, is metamorphic, which means it forms when limestone is subjected to great heat and pressure underground. In Renaissance times, the sculptor Michelangelo came here to choose the marble he required for his magnificent sculptures. He carved his masterpiece, the statue of David, from a block of Carrara marble that had been botched and left abandoned by another sculptor. Carrara marble, which polishes to a smooth, shiny finish, is still prized by sculptors today.

◄ Large blocks of finest marble stand ready for transport at a quarry in Carrara. The marble is traditionally used in sculpture, but it is also in demand in the construction industry.

▲ Salt is extracted from seawater at this plant near Bari. Water is allowed to flood shallow lakes, like this one. The water evaporates, leaving salt, which is raked into heaps.

MINERALS

Italy's stocks of minerals are also fairly scarce. Sicily, Sardinia, Tuscany, Lombardy and Piedmont are the chief mining areas. Iron ore, mercury, potash, zinc, lead, feldspar, pumice and barite are mined commercially. Pyrite, from volcanic areas in the south, is used in the chemical industry and to produce fertilizer and matches. The quarries of Carrara in Tuscany are famous for their marble (see page 27). Elsewhere in the country, granite is quarried. Salt is extracted from seawater on the Adriatic coast near Bari. With scant mineral reserves, Italy must import large quantities of iron ore and other materials it needs for industry.

FISHING, FORESTS AND FARMLAND

The long coastline is excellent for fishing, a traditional industry in Italy. The waters of the Adriatic and the shallow seas off Sicily provide the best fishing grounds. Tuna, sardines, swordfish and anchovies are among the main species caught commercially. In recent decades, long, floating drift nets have been set to catch fish that swim close to the surface. These nets have proved so efficient that stocks of fish have fallen sharply. The authorities have had to introduce quotas to control the number of fish that can be caught. Shellfish such as shrimps and mussels are also caught, as are squid and octopus. Fish and shellfish catches are consumed locally by Italians and by tourists. They are also canned or otherwise processed for sale abroad. Fish and shellfish have been reared in shallow lagoons along Italy's coast since Roman times. Today, the main species farmed commercially is the Mediterranean mussel.

Energy and Resources

After many centuries of felling, there is little forest left in Italy. The largest surviving forests grow in Abruzzi in central Italy, and Calabria and Puglia in the south. Native species in these forests include holm oak, beech and Aleppo and Corsican pines.

Some 53 per cent of Italy is used for agriculture: 15 per cent is pasture, while 38 per cent is arable. This farmland includes 26,980 sq km (10,520 sq miles) of irrigated land. The largest tracts of farmland lie in the north. Here, in the Lombardy plain and the Po valley, wheat, grapes, olives and sugar beet are grown. Beef and dairy cattle, pigs, chickens and sheep are also raised in many parts of Italy. However, Italy does not produce sufficient meat to meet its needs, and must import the rest, for example, beef from Argentina. The dry climate, poor, stony soil and steep terrain of the south hinder farming, but sheep and goats are pastured here. Durum (hard) wheat for pasta is also grown in the south. Terracing on the steep hillsides helps to prevent erosion.

 Did you know?

In Sicily, in an annual event called the *mattanza*, fishermen spread their nets in the shallows to catch large, meaty tuna as they arrive to spawn.

▼ Harvesting durum wheat in fields near Foggia in Puglia. This type of hard wheat is used to make pasta, a staple food of Italy.

CHAPTER 7

Economy and Income

Since the 1950s, Italy has seen a major shift from a largely agricultural to a highly industrialized economy. During the 1950s, Italy's economy grew rapidly, but it slowed during the 1960s. Despite some revival between 1970 and 2000, economic growth now stands at zero. In 2004, Italy had a workforce of 24.27 million, with unemployment estimated at 8.6 per cent, and the country ranked seventh in the world in terms of Gross National Income (GNI).

Italy is a leading producer of vehicles, clothing, machinery, iron and steel, chemicals, processed foods and ceramics. One reason for Italy's economic success since the Second World War has been its ability to combine new technology with a flair for design across a wide range of manufactured goods, from cars and computers to clothing and kettles.

WORKING CONDITIONS

Many Italian companies are small, family-run businesses employing fewer than one hundred

Focus on: FIAT

The car manufacturer, FIAT, is one of Italy's most successful companies and a major employer. In 1995, the company employed 145,000 people in Italy alone. It was founded in 1899, at the dawn of the motor car age. Based in Turin, the company now has factories elsewhere in Italy and in 50 countries worldwide. FIAT also owns vehicle manufacturers Lancia, Ferrari, Alfa Romeo and Masserati, which operate under their own names. In addition to cars, trucks and tractors, FIAT also makes aircraft engines, telecommunications equipment and heart pacemakers and is involved in insurance, property and publishing – owning one of Italy's best-selling newspapers, *La Stampa*.

 Did you know?

FIAT stands for *Fabbrica Italiana Automobile Torino* – the Italian Automobile Factory of Turin.

◀ Ports such as Castellammare di Stabia in the Bay of Naples have extensive shipyards. These were developed by the French occupiers in the eighteenth century and have been in use ever since.

people. However, there are also large companies, many of which are part-owned by the government. These include banks, steelworks, shipyards and car factories. In the second half of the twentieth century, the percentage of women in the workforce rose steadily, with large numbers of women working within service industries, but fewer working in industry. Wages are relatively low compared with other European nations – this is another reason why Italy has the edge over some of its competitors.

Unions are traditionally strong in Italy. Workers pay high taxes, but working conditions are generally good and pensions generous. However, a number of small businesses operate within the 'hidden economy'; this means they fail to register and thus avoid paying taxes. These businesses tend to pay low wages. Despite attempts to equalize industry and job opportunities throughout Italy, wages in the south lag behind those of the north, and there is higher unemployment in the south than there is in the north.

SERVICE INDUSTRIES AND AGRICULTURE

Service industries are the most important sector of the economy, employing 65 per cent of all workers and producing 69 per cent of the GNI in 2004. The service sector includes jobs in government, trade, finance, transport and social services. Retailing and hotels and restaurants, boosted by tourism, are a major money-earner. The tourist industry is geared towards foreign and Italian holidaymakers (see pages 52-3).

▲ Tourism is an important earner in beautiful areas such as the island of Capri. Boat excursions are popular in many resorts.

Economic data

- Gross National Income (GNI) in US$: 1,503,562,000,000
- World rank by GNI: 7
- GNI per capita in US$: 26,120
- World rank by GNI per capita: 26
- Economic growth: 0%

Source: World Bank

During the 1950s, around 33 per cent of all Italy's workers were involved in agriculture. By 2004, only 5.5 per cent of workers were employed in agriculture, which produced just 3 per cent of the GNI. Italy's main crops include wheat, maize, rice, sugar beet, olives, and grapes for winemaking. Many regions of Italy are known for their wines, with climate and soil suiting different grapes. Italy is the world's leading producer of tomatoes and tomato products. Fruits and vegetables grown here include cherries, apples, peaches, oranges, potatoes, soya beans and globe artichokes.

INDUSTRY AND MANUFACTURING

In 2004, industry (including manufacturing, construction and mining) employed 29.5 per cent of workers and yielded 28 per cent of the GNI. Despite the government's attempt to kick-start manufacturing in the south, Italy's industrial heartland remains the north, particularly in and around the cities of Turin, Milan and Genoa. Craft industries producing leather goods, glass and ceramics date back to medieval times, and different cities are known for characteristic products: leather from Naples, jewellery from Florence, and glass from the island of Murano in Venice.

Italy is a leader in the world of fashion, including clothing, shoes, perfume and accessories (see box opposite). Since the 1950s, top manufacturers have employed cutting-edge designers to create stylish but highly functional goods, including furniture and tableware. Italy is also a top vehicle manufacturer, with FIAT known for family cars (see page 30), Ferrari, Alfa Romeo and Lamborghini for sports and racing cars, Vespa for scooters and Ducati for motorbikes. Italy also produces aircraft and vehicle parts, including tyres by Pirelli. Electronic goods, such as computers, are manufactured in Italy (notably by Olivetti). Zanussi, Delonghi and others produce domestic appliances, such as refrigerators, cookers and washing machines.

◀ Many Italians prefer to buy fruit and vegetables from market stalls or small, family-run grocery shops rather than large supermarket chains. This greengrocer's shop is in Sorrento.

Economy and Income 33

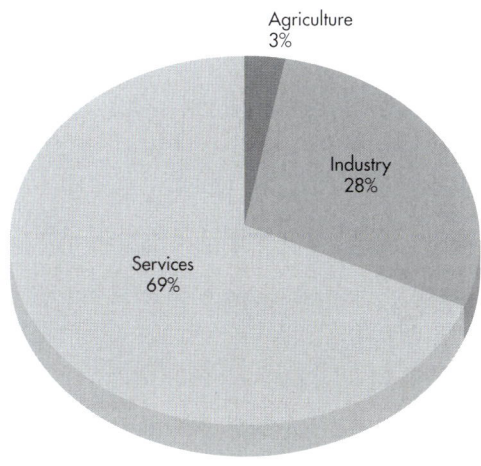

▲ Contribution by sector to national income

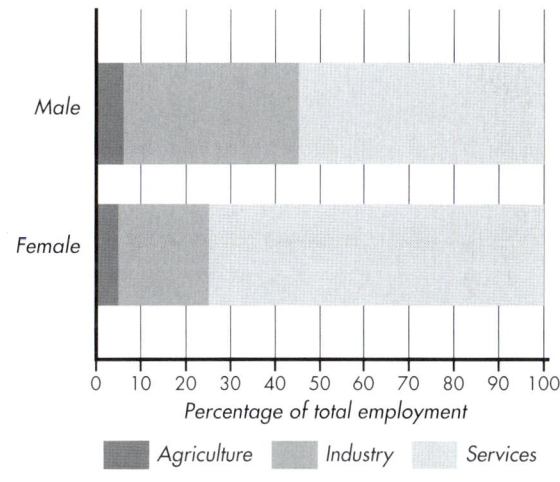

▲ Labour force by sector and gender

Focus on: Fashion

Italy is one of the world's fashion capitals, with names such as Gucci, Armani, Prada, Versace and Benetton known internationally. The fashion industry is mainly based in Milan. Italian people have a reputation for being very fashion conscious, with northerners in particular known for their love of designer clothes. Benetton began as a small, family-run business in 1965, and now owns a chain of shops worldwide. The house of Armani, founded in 1975, produces designer clothing, as well as perfume and accessories. Twice yearly the fashion houses launch their new collections on the catwalks of Milan, Paris, London and New York.

◄ Top models show off the latest collection by Italian designer Donatella Versace at a fashion show in Milan.

CHAPTER 8

Global Connections

From medieval times, Italian city-states forged links with other European nations through trade and finance. Further links were political: parts of Italy became colonies of foreign nations such as France, Austria and Spain. In the early 1900s, Italy itself colonized Somalia, Eritrea, Libya and later Ethiopia. This forged new connections, some of which still influence modern trade patterns, for example, Libya supplies Italy with oil.

ECONOMIC AND POLITICAL TIES

In 1957, Italy was among the six founding members of the European Economic Community (EEC). The EEC's main purpose was to ease trade among its European members by removing import and export duties. In 1992, the EEC was renamed the European Union (EU) and had 15 member states. In 2004 it expanded again, to 25 member states. In addition to enjoying free trade, EU members work for closer political ties. However, to date, Italy, along with most other EU countries, has stopped short of adopting the European constitution, which would represent a further step on the road to union.

EU money has helped to regenerate industry in southern Italy, for example, by providing grants for poor farmers. As EU citizens, Italians are now free to work anywhere within the EU. In 2002, Italy abandoned its national currency, the

▼ Goods are unloaded from a bulk cargo vessel at Salerno port, a major cargo port for southern Italy.

lira, in favour of the single European currency, the Euro. Many Italians believe that economic targets set by the EU have forced Italian governments to take a more disciplined approach to the economy. This has helped to keep inflation and interest rates low. However, the Euro is not popular with everyone in Italy (partly because prices rose when the Euro was adopted), and recently there have been calls to bring back the lira.

Italy is a member of many other international organizations besides the EU. They include the United Nations (UN) and NATO (the North Atlantic Treaty Organization). In the early 2000s, Italy has worked closely with other UN and NATO members to maintain international peace and security following the rise of Islamic terrorism and the bombing of the World Trade Center in New York City on 11 September 2001.

▲ Italian troops were among the forces involved in the war in Iraq in 2003. Here two Italian soldiers walk in front of a military police base that has been destroyed in a suicide bomb attack.

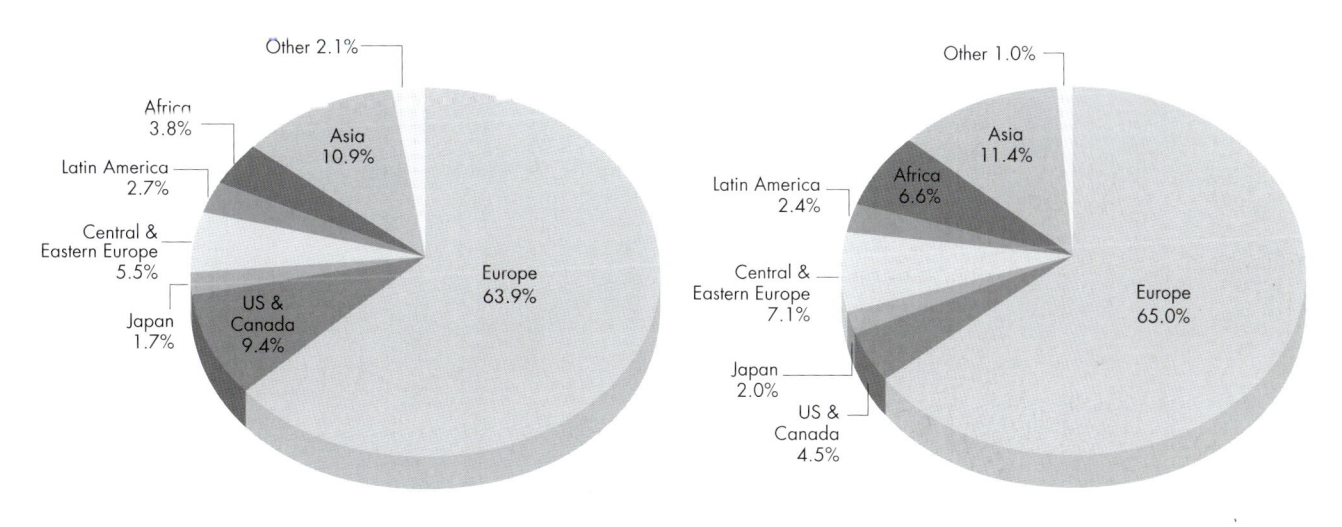

▲ Destination of exports by major trading region

- Europe 63.9%
- Asia 10.9%
- US & Canada 9.4%
- Central & Eastern Europe 5.5%
- Africa 3.8%
- Latin America 2.7%
- Other 2.1%
- Japan 1.7%

▲ Origin of imports by major trading region

- Europe 65.0%
- Asia 11.4%
- Central & Eastern Europe 7.1%
- Africa 6.6%
- US & Canada 4.5%
- Latin America 2.4%
- Japan 2.0%
- Other 1.0%

▲ The Italian obsession with coffee is legendary, and over the years Italian habits and customs – and coffee-shops – have travelled to many parts of the world, including here in South Korea.

TRADING PARTNERS

Much of Italy's trade is done within Europe, with 63.9 per cent of exports and 65 per cent of imports passing to and from other EU members. Trade with the USA is also important. Italy's main exports are machinery and equipment, clothing, shoes, vehicles, chemicals, food and drink. Italy's chief imports are machinery, oil, vehicles, chemicals, minerals and food, which chiefly come from Germany, France, the UK, the Netherlands and the USA.

Since the 1980s, Italy has spent more on its imports than it has made from its exports, resulting in a trade deficit (shortfall). The shortfall has also been caused by the rising price of oil, which is imported to provide energy. Foreign currency from the tourist industry helps to offset the imbalance.

Italian trade connections include those of the Mafia, which has unofficial links with other nations, smuggling and trafficking in illegal drugs. In recent years, the Italian government has tried to crack down on the 'informal sector', which can involve all sorts of activities, from unlicensed but otherwise legal street trading to international drugs trafficking. The taxes raised from bringing legal informal businesses within the formal sector would make a substantial contribution to the economy.

Did you know?

Between 1861 and 1973, some 26 million Italians emigrated abroad.

EMIGRATION AND IMMIGRATION

Since the unification of Italy in the 1860s, millions of Italians have emigrated to other countries, including Germany, Switzerland and the Americas. Italians, especially from the south, have left in search of work and a better life. The early 1900s saw a huge number of Italian emigrants settling in US cities such as New York and Boston, and in Latin American countries such as Argentina and Brazil. Emigration peaked in the 1950s and 1960s, with 390,000 leaving in 1961 alone.

The early 1970s saw a shift, with more immigrants arriving in Italy than emigrants leaving the country. Some of the arrivals were Italians returning home having made money abroad. Others were from Eastern Europe and North Africa, where living standards were lower than in Italy. Like other nations, Italy sets quotas to limit the number of immigrants entering the country legally. However, many refugees from nations bordering the Mediterranean take advantage of Italy's long coastline to enter illegally. In 1990-1 and again in 1997, waves of Albanian refugees fled to Italy to escape political crisis or war, and 1992 saw a flood of refugees from the former Yugoslavia, fleeing war.

◀ Italian-American communities in the USA celebrate traditional Catholic feast days. Here Italian-Americans in Manhattan celebrate the festival of San Gennaro.

Focus on: Italian-American communities

New York, Boston and many other US cities have Italian neighbourhoods. These are the legacy of the early 1900s, when large numbers of Italians arrived to begin a new life in the USA. Such neighbourhoods have stores selling Italian foods, and there are Italian societies, and Catholic church services held in Italian. Original (or first-generation) Italian immigrants spoke little English, but their children were taught English at school. Third- and fourth-generation Italians may speak very little Italian, and only their surnames reveal their origins.

CHAPTER 9

Transport and Communications

Italy's long, narrow shape and mountainous terrain present difficulties for land travel. Sicily, Sardinia and the smaller islands are, of course, isolated by sea. Nevertheless, Italy's transport and communications networks are well developed and generally efficient. Between the 1950s and mid-1980s, the *Cassa per il Mezzogiorno* (see page 20) improved transport and communications in the south.

ROAD AND RAIL

Italy's 479,688 km (298,072 miles) of roads are all paved, and include 6,940 km (4,300 miles) of *autostrada* – motorway. Between 1955 and 1975, a major road-building programme was carried out largely by private companies, so road users are charged tolls on certain roads, for example, motorways. Routes such as the Simplon Pass and the Mont Blanc tunnel cut through the Alps, and link Italy with France, Switzerland and Austria to the north, while the *Autostrada del Sol* (Highway of the Sun) links northern and southern Italy.

Did you know?

In 1924, Italy began building the world's first toll motor highway. The highway linked Milan with Varese to the north.

▼ High-speed trains provide fast connections between certain Italian cities, for example, Milan and Rome.

Transport and Communications

With about one in every two Italians a car-owner, city roads are congested during rush hours. Flyovers ease congestion, while noisy scooters and small cars navigate narrow streets. Many people travel to work or school by public transport – either by bus, train, coach or tram, or by metro in Rome and Milan.

Italian railways are state owned, subsidized and inexpensive to use. There are frequent services, and many people consider this the best way to travel about Italy. The rail network includes around 19,319 km (12,005 miles) of track, of which some 12,000 km are electrified. Under Mussolini, the network was improved and magnificent stations, such as Milan, were built. High-speed trains can cover the 1,320 km (819 miles) from Milan to Reggio di Calabria at the tip of Italy in 11 hours. However, Italian trains are notorious for their lack of punctuality, and many journeys involve long delays.

AIR AND WATER TRANSPORT

Historically, the sea offered an effective means of travel between coastal cities. Although it is not as speedy as travel overland, sea transportation is still used extensively in Italy today. Italy has fifteen major seaports, including Genoa, Trieste, Naples, Bari, and Augusta in Sicily. Many oil tankers dock at either Genoa or at Porto Foxi in Sardinia, while La Spezia in the north-west is mainly a container port.

▶ Electric buses provide efficient inner-city transport in centres such as Naples, shown here.

Transport & communications data

- Total roads: 479,688 km/298,072 miles
- Total paved roads: 479,688 km/298,072 miles
- Total unpaved roads: 0 km/0 miles
- Total railways: 19,319 km/12,005 miles
- Airports: 134
- Cars per 1,000 people: 542
- Mobile phones per 1,000 people: 1,018
- Personal computers per 1,000 people: 231
- Internet users per 1,000 people: 337

Source: World Bank and CIA World Factbook

Ferries and hydrofoils link the mainland with offshore islands and with France, Greece and Turkey. The Po is the only major navigable river, with canals leading to the northern lakes. The only means of travel within the city of Venice is by water (see box below).

Air travel is the quickest way of covering long distances on the Italian peninsula. Of the 134 airports listed in 2004, over one hundred have paved runways. All major cities have airports, with many operating international flights. Leonard da Vinci airport at Fiumicino, near Rome, and Linate and Malpensa, near Milan, are the busiest airports. The national airline, Alitalia, is largely government owned.

COMMUNICATIONS AND MEDIA

Italy has highly developed communications systems, with fast, fully automated telephone, fax and data services. In 2003, there were 26.6 million land telephones. Mobile phone use has risen rapidly since 1995, when only a small

Focus on: Transport in Venice

With no roads, railway or metro in Venice, the only way to get about is by boat or on foot. This famous city was founded in the fifth century and lies just offshore in the north-east of the country. It is made up of 117 islands, linked by 400 bridges, and was originally built on wooden stilts driven into the mud. Venice's 'streets' are 150 canals. People travel about the city centre by *vaporetto* (waterbus) or *motoscafo* (launch). Venice's famous gondolas offer expensive tourist rides, but specific types of gondola are also used to collect rubbish, deliver goods and for funerals.

◀ Gondolas and other boat traffic dock at piers like this one in Venice. This view of the Church of Santa Maria della Salute is a favourite with artists and photographers.

percentage of Italians had mobiles; now there is one mobile phone per person. Internet use is also increasing quickly, although the number of Internet hosts, 1.25 million in 2005, is fairly low for a nation with advanced technology. Although only one in five Italians owned a personal computer in 2002, at least a third of the population used the Internet.

Italy's state broadcasting company, RAI, has three channels which tend to represent different political viewpoints. Silvio Berlusconi's media empire, Fininvest, operates three further channels, including the popular Canale 5. In addition to three state-run radio stations, there are thousands of local and privately owned stations. Half of all Italians own a TV, and there is one radio per person. There are some seventy daily newspapers, owned either by political parties, the Church or large businesses, and many of them therefore offer a particular political outlook. The most popular daily newspapers are Rome's *La Repubblica*, Milan's *Corriere della Sera*, and Turin's *La Stampa*. There are also numerous magazines, mostly dedicated to particular interests, such as sport and fashion.

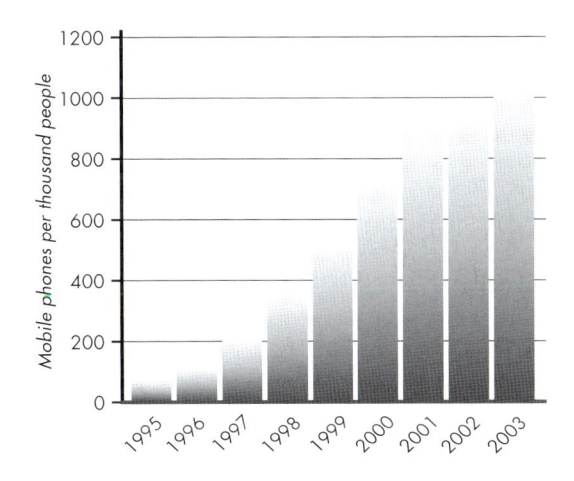

▲ Mobile phone use, 1995-2003

Focus on: Pioneers of telecommunications

In the early days of telecommunications, Italians led the way with many pioneering inventions. In the 1850s, Giovanni Caselli invented the *pantelegrafo*, a device that was a forerunner of modern fax machines. In 1871, Antonio Meucci designed an early telephone; however, later in the decade, Scottish-born Alexander Graham Bell patented the invention. Guglielmo Marconi was a pioneer of radio who sent the first radio signals across the Atlantic from Newfoundland to Britain.

◄ Mobile phones are popular particularly with younger people in Italy, as elsewhere in the world.

CHAPTER 10

Education and Health

Education and, particularly, health are high priorities in Italy. In 2002, Italy spent 4.7 per cent of its Gross Domestic Product (GDP) on education. It spent 8.5 per cent of its GDP on health – a proportion higher than that of the UK, but lower than that of the USA.

Some 98.5 per cent of Italians over the age of 15 can read and write. Literacy is slightly higher among men than women, reflecting past attitudes to gender and schooling. In the past, more boys than girls continued in secondary education, but this is no longer the case.

PRIMARY AND SECONDARY EDUCATION

In Italy, education is free and compulsory for all children between the ages of six and 14. Many children go to nursery school between the ages of three and five. Ninety per cent of children go to state-run schools. Compulsory schooling is split into five years of primary education and three years of middle school (*scuola media*). This may be followed by four or five years of optional senior secondary education, which can take the form of study at a technical or teacher-training school, or an arts- or science-orientated course at a *liceo*, or college. Italy's education system is currently being overhauled to bring it into line with other EU countries. This will extend the age of free, compulsory schooling to 16. In 2002, 100 per cent of children attended primary school and 88 per cent attended secondary school. Forty-one per cent of students continued their studies at college or university.

▼ A lesson in progress in a class at a primary school in Rome.

Class sizes are small in Italy; there was one teacher for every 10.8 primary school pupils in 2001. The school day is fairly short, with classes from 8-8.30 am to 1.30-2 pm. The school year runs from September to June. Pupils who gain poor results must repeat a year before continuing with their education. This affects about 11 per cent of girls, but more than 20 per cent of boys.

HIGHER EDUCATION

Senior secondary school graduates may attend university, but some courses are so popular that would-be students must take an entrance exam. Italy has 45 public universities, of which Rome is the largest with over 170,000 students. There are also private universities, many of which are run by the Catholic Church. University enrolment has risen steadily since the 1960s, with 1.25 million students now in higher education each year.

Did you know?

The University of Bologna in north-central Italy is among the world's oldest universities, dating from the eleventh century.

Focus on: The national curriculum

Italy has introduced a national curriculum, to standardize education across the country and ensure all students are well prepared for exams. The government's Ministry of Education is responsible for setting educational priorities and selecting coursework books. Middle school pupils study geography, mathematics, science, history and civic education, Italian, art, and a foreign language. Senior secondary school students follow an arts, classics, language or science-based course, or major in vocational training (for example, teacher training).

Education and health

- Life expectancy at birth male: 76.9
- Life expectancy at birth female: 82.9
- Infant mortality rate per 1,000: 4
- Under five mortality rate per 1,000: 4
- Physicians per 1,000 people: 6.1
- Health expenditure as % of GDP: 8.5%
- Education expenditure as % of GDP: 4.7%
- Primary net enrolment: 100%
- Pupil-teacher ratio, primary: 10.8
- Adult literacy as % age 15+: 98.5

Source: United Nations Agencies and World Bank

◀ Chinese students at Bologna University – one of Europe's oldest centres of learning.

University tuition fees are quite low, but students do not receive grants for living expenses. Many students remain at home with their parents to avoid paying rent. They work part-time to cover their living expenses, which means they take longer to complete their degrees. Since the 1960s, the number of women in higher education has risen steadily, but unemployment is higher among female graduates than it is among males.

HEALTH

Standards of medical care in Italy are generally good. The national health plan provides low-cost medical care for all citizens. With one doctor for every 227 patients, Italy has a high doctor to patient ratio. Most Italians eat a healthy diet, with plenty of fresh fruit and vegetables. Pasta is central to the Italian diet. In general, Italians eat fewer processed foods that are high in fat and sugar than people in many other western countries.

Infant mortality is low in Italy, with just four deaths for every 1,000 live births in 2003. The death rate for children under five is also low, with four deaths for every 1,000. Life expectancy at birth rose steadily in Italy in the late twentieth century, as a result of improvements in public health and sanitation and continuing advances in medical science. In 1960, the average life expectancy at birth was 69.1 years, rising to 73.9 in 1980, and to 79.8 in 2003. As is the case elsewhere in the world,

▼ A doctor attends an elderly patient at his home in Basilicata, a poor part of the south.

Education and Health

women live somewhat longer than men. Average life expectancy in 2003 was 82.9 years for women and 76.9 years for men.

As people live longer, the increasing number of older people puts more and more pressure on Italy's health system. Changes are being made to cope with the growing demand from older people. Traditionally, older people were looked after by their families, but this is changing as more women are in paid employment, working outside the home.

The major causes of death in Italy are cancer and heart disease. In 2005 there were an estimated 10.3 deaths for every 1,000 people – similar to other nations in Western Europe. The number of deaths per thousand actually rose slightly in the 1990s, but has since fallen again. HIV/AIDS affected an estimated 0.5 per cent of the population in 2005, with an estimated 100 deaths from AIDS in 2003.

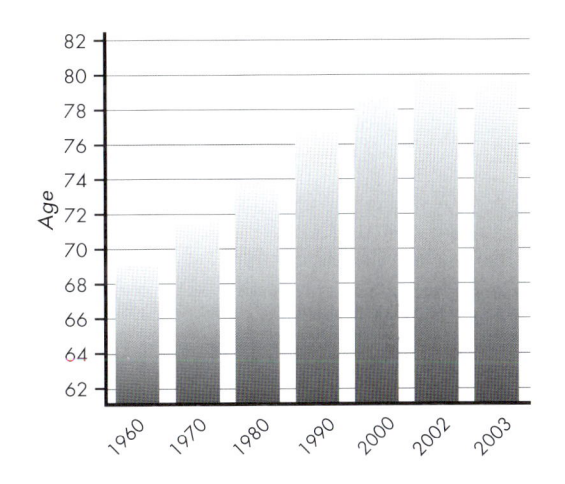

▲ Life expectancy at birth, 1960-2003

▲ The Italian diet consists of a relatively healthy balance of fresh foods, including meat, which provides protein, and carbohydrates such as pasta and bread. Italians also eat lots of fresh vegetables and salads.

CHAPTER 11

Culture and Religion

Italy is internationally renowned for its great artistic achievements, particularly dating from the Renaissance, but continuing into modern times. As the home of the pope, it is the spiritual heartland of Roman Catholics throughout the world.

ART AND LITERATURE

The word 'renaissance' means 'rebirth'. During the Renaissance, from the fourteenth to sixteenth centuries, classical arts and learning were revived and new art forms evolved. Great Renaissance artists include Giotto (lived around 1267-1337), Sandro Botticelli (1444-1510) and Raphael (1483-1520). Michelangelo (1475-1564) was a Florentine sculptor, painter, architect and poet. His sculpture, *David*, and his frescos in the Sistine Chapel in Rome are masterpieces of the depiction of the human form. Michelangelo's contemporary, Leonardo da Vinci (1452-1519), produced one of the world's most famous images, the *Mona Lisa*. Leonardo was also a great scientist and engineer. Some of Italy's best-known literary figures also date from Renaissance times. The poets Dante, Petrarch and Giovanni Boccaccio all produced great works, including the epic poem *The Divine Comedy* (by Dante), which describes a journey through hell and purgatory to heaven, and *The Decameron* (by Boccaccio), a collection of short stories.

The Baroque period followed the Renaissance and saw the work of painter, architect and sculptor, Giovanni Lorenzo Bernini (1598-1680), and dramatic religious paintings and portraits by the Venetian artist Titian (1490-1576).

The twentieth century produced new, dynamic art movements, including Futurism and, in the 1960s, the Art of the Poor. Twentieth-century Italian poets include Salvatore Quasimodo (1901-68), while modern novelists include Dario Fo, Primo Levi and Umberto Eco, who wrote the novel *The Name of the Rose*.

◀ Some modern Italian artists draw inspiration from the landscape, while others produce abstract or conceptual art. This artist is working on a classic Italian street scene in Sorrento.

MUSIC

Italians are justly proud of their musical heritage. Early composers, such as Giovanni Palestrina (lived around 1525-94), Claudio Monteverdi (around 1567-1643) and Antonio Vivaldi (around 1678-1741), wrote beautiful church music. The nineteenth century was the golden age of Italian opera, with Gioacchino Rossini (1792-1868), Gaetano Donizetti (1797-1848), Giuseppe Verdi (1813-1901) and Giacomo Puccini (1858-1924) all composing great works. Every major Italian city has an opera house – La Scala in Milan is the most famous. During the latter part of the twentieth century, the tenor singer, Luciano Pavarotti, helped to revive interest in opera worldwide.

Italy is also renowned for filmmaking. An important and influential era of Italian filmmaking was neo-realism, which refers to a period during the 1940s when directors such as Luchino Visconti, Vittorio De Sica and Roberto Rossellini made films working in real locations and using local people as well as professional actors. Films such as *Ossessione* (Visconti), *The Bicycle Thieves* (De Sica) and *Stromboli* (Rossellini) focused on human problems in natural settings. In the 1960s, 'spaghetti Westerns' (so-called because they were Italian-made) caught the public imagination. Italian filmmaker Sergio Leone directed three films, beginning with *For a Fistful of Dollars*, which made an international star of US actor Clint Eastwood. Acclaimed Italian film directors of more recent times include Bernardo Bertolucci (*The Last Emperor*) and Roberto Benigni (*The Postman* and *Life is Beautiful*).

Did you know?

The terms commonly used in written music are Italian, for example, *piano* (soft), *forte* (loud), *lento* (slow), *andante* (moderate walking pace) and *con brio* (lively).

▼ The audience settles down for an opera performance at the Roman amphitheatre in Verona.

RELIGION

In 1985, a public referendum decided that Roman Catholicism was no longer to be Italy's state religion; nevertheless, it is still the dominant faith. In 2004, 79.9 per cent of Italians were Roman Catholics and some 1.2 per cent followed Islam (most Muslims were immigrants from North and West Africa). Another 2.3 per cent followed other religions, including Protestantism and Judaism. The remaining 16.6 per cent stated they had no religion.

Despite official statistics, the number of practising Catholics is falling in Italy. Some 97 per cent of Italians are baptized, but only about one in three of this group attends church services regularly. Some sources put this figure as low as one in ten. The number of young people entering religious orders has also fallen steeply. However, the parish priest remains a respected member of the community, especially in rural areas, where faith is often stronger than in the cities.

In the past, the Catholic Church exerted great influence on social values in Italy. However, the Church's influence in the country has waned in recent decades. Catholic doctrine opposes abortion, divorce and artificial methods of birth control. However, in 1970 the Italian government voted to permit divorce and, in a 1978 referendum, Italians voted to legalize abortion. The low birth rate suggests that most people in Italy practise birth control.

Focus on: The Vatican City

The Vatican City, occupying less than 0.5 sq km (0.2 sq miles) in Rome, is the headquarters of the Catholic Church, which has over 850 million followers worldwide. This tiny, independent state has its own diplomatic corps and security force (the Swiss Guard) with 120 men. Rome has been Catholicism's base ever since St Peter, the first pope, was buried there in ancient times.

◀ A view from the roof of St Peter's Basilica over the Vatican City and Rome. The Vatican houses masterpieces by Renaissance artists such as Raphael and Michelangelo.

◀ The south is the stronghold of Catholicism in Italy. Here the people of Calabria celebrate the feast of the Virgin Mary with a procession.

FESTIVALS

The Church's influence is still strong in terms of tradition and festivals. Most national holidays are Catholic feast days. In addition to Christmas and Easter, these include Epiphany, All Saints' Day, the Assumption and the Immaculate Conception. These last two honour the Virgin Mary. Easter is preceded by Lent, a period of fasting that lasts 40 days during which, traditionally, meat is not eaten. The word carnival comes from the Italian *carne vale*, meaning 'meat, farewell'. Just before Lent, carnivals in Rome, Venice and elsewhere are held, with people parading through the streets wearing masks and costumes.

In addition to national festivals, every town and village has its own patron saint, with feast days marked with processions and celebrations. Some of these festivities incorporate customs dating back to medieval or even Roman times. The city of Siena is home to a twice-yearly horse race held to honour the Virgin Mary. Riders in medieval costume race bareback around Siena's main square.

THE VATICAN

In the eighth century, the Frankish king, Charlemagne, gave a huge tract of land to the pope, and this formed the basis of the Papal States. In addition to this vast territory, popes also wielded immense spiritual and political influence throughout medieval times and beyond. During the 1860s, the papacy opposed Italy's unification, and the Papal States were the last region to become part of Italy in 1870. After this, popes retreated to the Vatican. In 1929, under Mussolini, the Lateral Treaty formalized relations between Church and state, and the Vatican became an independent country. In 2005, Pope Benedict XVI became the 264th successor to St Peter.

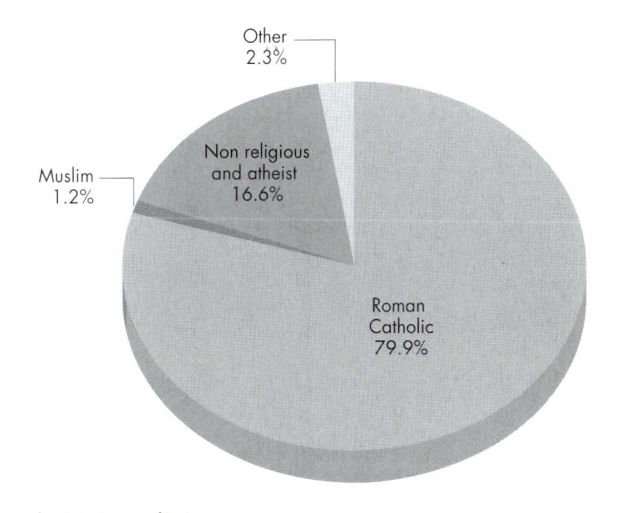

▲ Major religions

- Roman Catholic 79.9%
- Non religious and atheist 16.6%
- Muslim 1.2%
- Other 2.3%

Leisure and Tourism

With four to six weeks' paid holiday a year, Italians have more time off than workers in many countries. The warm, sunny climate allows Italians to make the most of their leisure time. It also makes Italy a popular destination for foreign tourists.

FAMILY CUSTOMS

The family lies at the heart of Italian culture and everyday life. Traditionally, elderly people have tended to live with their grown-up children and grandchildren. However, this practice is becoming less common, especially in big cities where life is less traditional than in rural areas. In Italian culture, the mother and son are the focus of the family. Many sons remain at home until they reach their thirties, with their mothers attending to their every need. However, when men marry, they may find that their wives are less willing to perform this role since they also go out to work. Popular songs are written in praise of mothers, and Italians even have a name for their national devotion to the idea of the mother, *mammismo*.

FOOD

Italian mothers have a reputation for being wonderful cooks, and Italians generally are passionate about food, as are the many visitors who sample real Italian cooking. Italian food is one of the world's most popular cuisines. One of the country's most famous dishes, pizza, is usually eaten as a light meal, followed by a dessert of ice cream, one of Italy's most famous inventions. Italians are renowned for their love

▼ Pizza is baked in an oven in the kitchen of a modern restaurant in Vico Equense near Naples. In many restaurants, pizza is still baked in traditional brick-lined ovens.

of coffee, with many different types including *espresso*, *cappuccino* and *caffelatte*. Pasta, made from wheat, comes in many shapes and sizes, including spirals, shells, curls and ribbons, and of course, *spaghetti*, which means 'little strings'.

Italians usually buy their ingredients fresh from the many excellent markets. Shops open in the morning and early evening, and close between 1pm and 4pm to avoid the hottest part of the day. The main meal, traditionally enjoyed at midday, is now generally eaten in the evening. It consists of several courses, of which *antipasti* or appetisers, such as cooked meats or salad, are the first. Next is a course of pasta, soup or risotto, followed by the main dish of meat or fish, accompanied or followed by vegetables.

Then comes cheese and/or fresh fruit and dessert. All this may be washed down with a fine Italian wine.

LEISURE ACTIVITIES

Italy's mild climate means that people spend much of their leisure time outdoors, perhaps enjoying a game of *bocce* (bowls) or a drink in the local café. The evening stroll, or *passeggiata*, provides a chance to gossip with friends and show off new clothes. In towns and cities, Italians enjoy evening concerts and plays, and people from all walks of life (not merely the rich) attend the opera. Italians are also keen cinemagoers, although in recent decades television has caused a drop-off in cinema attendances.

Did you know?

Pasta did not originate in Italy. The Venetian merchant and traveller, Marco Polo, brought it back from China to Italy during the thirteenth century.

▼ Onlookers watch the world go by during the evening *passeggiata* in the coastal resort of Sabaudia, not far from Rome.

SPORT

Italy is a nation of sports enthusiasts. Italians love both watching and playing sport and football is often said to be a national obsession. Milan, Turin and Rome have two major league teams apiece: Milan is home to AC and Intermilan, Turin is the base for Torino and Juventus, and Roma and Lazio are located in Rome. The national team, nicknamed the *azzurri* (blues), arouses great enthusiasm. Italy has won the World Cup three times, most recently in Spain in 1982.

Cycling has a big following, with the key race, the *Giro d'Italia* (Tour of Italy) taking place in May or June. Italy has two Formula 1 circuits, and motor racing is popular (Italy is a leading manufacturer of racing cars). Basketball, volleyball and baseball are played, along with watersports, such as swimming, rowing and yachting. Italians also enjoy skiing and snowboarding in the mountains.

HOLIDAYS AND TOURISM

Most Italians take at least two weeks of their annual holiday in summer – usually in August. At this time, many shops and factories in inland cities close, and traffic jams occur during the mass exodus and return. Over 80 per cent of Italians holiday within their own country, heading for the coast or mountains, for example, the Alps. However, foreign tourism is becoming increasingly popular and more than 26 million Italians travelled abroad as tourists in 2003.

Tourism is an important industry in Italy, bringing in 8.9 per cent of foreign earnings in 2003. Tourism also provides employment, although many jobs in hotels, restaurants and shops are only seasonal. The number of foreign tourists visiting Italy rose in the late 1990s, peaked in 2000 and has dropped off slightly since then. Nearly half of all foreign visitors head for Venice, and nearly a quarter visit the major historic cities of Venice, Florence and Rome.

◀ In summer, the Italian mountains are a magnet for coach tours, and for more active visitors such as hikers, climbers and mountain-bikers.

Leisure and Tourism 53

◀ The famous leaning tower of Pisa is now in danger of collapse. Conservation efforts are focused on shoring up the unstable ground on which the tower is built.

Among the many attractions are art galleries such as the Uffizi in Florence, and historic sites dating from ancient or Renaissance times, including the Roman town of Pompeii near Naples, the Greek temples in Sicily, and the great cathedrals. Coastal resorts such as Portofino in the north-west, Rimini on the Adriatic and Amalfi and Capri further south are popular with Italians and foreigners. While vital to the economy, tourism also causes problems, including congestion and pollution. Uncontrolled development has spoiled some stretches of the Italian coast.

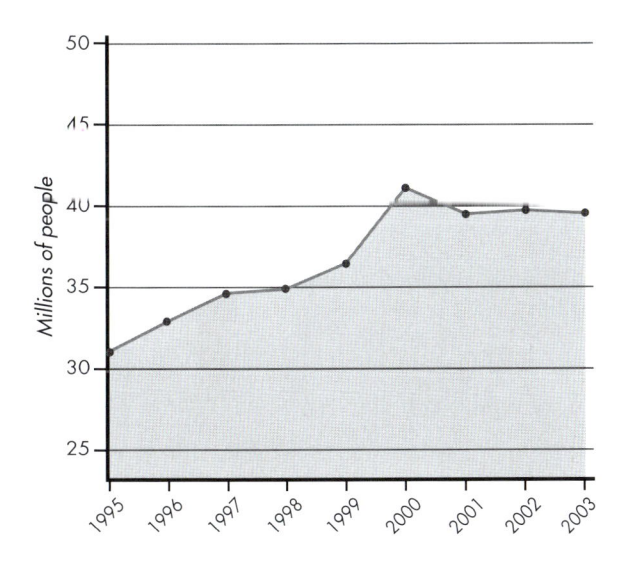

▲ Changes in international tourism, 1990-2003

Tourism in Italy

- Tourist arrivals, millions: 39.604
- Earnings from tourism in US$: 32,565,999,616
- Tourism as % foreign earnings: 8.9
- Tourist departures, millions: 26.817
- Expenditure on tourism in US$: 23,723,999,232

Source: World Bank

Did you know?

The Leaning Tower of Pisa is a major tourist attraction. Subsidence caused the tower to lean soon after construction began in 1173.

CHAPTER 13

Environment and Conservation

Land, air and water pollution are all problems in Italy, especially in densely populated and highly industrialized areas. Wild habitats are disappearing, and, although national parks help to protect the nation's wildlife, some of this is under threat.

AIR AND WATER POLLUTION

In built-up areas, exhaust from traffic and emissions from industry cause air pollution. Cities such as Bologna and Milan have closed some of their central areas to traffic in an effort to curb pollution and congestion, while Naples and Florence have introduced buses that run on cleaner fuels, such as LPG. Waste gases from cars, cities and power stations also mix with water vapour in the air to produce acid rain, which damages historic buildings.

Acid rain also kills trees and wildlife in lakes and rivers and is a particular problem in the northern industrial areas. Since the 1980s, the government has introduced laws to curb the release of waste gases.

As a highly industrialized nation, Italy burns large amounts of fossil fuel, and so adds to the release of carbon dioxide (CO_2) and other gases that contribute towards global warming. Warming weather worldwide is causing sea levels to rise, which in future may threaten low-lying cities such as Venice (see box opposite). Italy has signed the Kyoto Protocol, an

▼ This electric car, made by the Italian company Start Lab, helps to improve urban environments. Its small size eases congestion and parking difficulties.

international agreement to reduce CO_2 emissions, and the government has set targets for reducing emissions.

Italy's rivers and surrounding seas are polluted by waste from towns, factories and agriculture. The Mediterranean is one of the world's most polluted seas, and the Adriatic is one of the worst affected areas. Pesticides and fertilizers used in farming run off the land into rivers such as the Po and discharge into coastal waters, causing algae (microscopic plants) to multiply. This so-called algae bloom reduces oxygen levels in the water, harming aquatic life; it is also unsightly and smelly, which puts off tourists. Italy is party to several treaties to restrict the dumping of waste at sea, but agricultural run-off is difficult to regulate.

Focus on: Venice in peril

The city of Venice is under threat. Its historic buildings are slowly but surely sinking into the lagoon on which the city is sited. Pollutants in seawater are eating away at foundations, and buildings are also damaged by the waves caused by passing boats. In winter, when very high tides occur, seawater floods parts of the city, including St Mark's Square with its ancient and beautiful buildings. The worst floods have struck in 1966, 1979 and 1986. Many solutions have been proposed, of which the most practical may be to build a barrage (barrier) across the lagoon entrances, to protect against very high tides.

▲ Tourists wade barefoot across a flooded St Mark's Square in Venice after autumn rains and high tides caused the water level of the Venetian lagoon to rise.

THREATS TO LAND AND SOIL

In past years, Italy disposed of huge amounts of domestic waste in pits called landfill sites. Now a shortage of such sites is causing a crisis in waste disposal here, as elsewhere in Europe. The Italian government encourages recycling to reduce the amount of waste. Italy's record on recycling is one of the best in the world. Around half of all used paper and glass is recycled.

Over the last 2,000 years, most of the ancient forests that once covered Italy have been felled. Without the roots of trees and other plants to keep the soil in place, the land quickly becomes eroded. Deforestation and overgrazing by livestock have led to erosion on steep hillsides. In 1996, a landslide into the Bay of Naples damaged property and killed five people. One way to tackle erosion is to plant more trees. Much of the 23 per cent of Italy that is covered by forests has been fairly recently planted. Another way to limit erosion is to reduce the number of livestock grazing in steep areas.

In general, wetlands absorb moisture and so help prevent flooding. The draining of wetlands to create new land for industry and farming has increased the risk of floods in Italy. In 1966, priceless artworks in Florence were ruined when the River Arno burst its banks. The worst floods in recent decades struck Piedmont and Liguria in 1994.

▼ An Italian woman recycles used glass bottles at a bank in Naples. Recycling centres like this one are now in use all over Italy.

WILDLIFE AND CONSERVATION

Italy's spectacular wildlife includes golden eagles, bears, wolves and lynx in remote mountains, and wild boar and mouflon sheep (a type of wild mountain sheep) on Sardinia. However, Italian wildlife is under threat for several reasons, of which habitat loss is the most important. Over the centuries, grasslands, forests, marshes and even remote uplands have been cleared to make way for new farms, industrial sites, roads and suburbs. Very little natural vegetation is left in areas such as the Po valley.

Mammals such as deer and boar are threatened by the Italians' enthusiasm for hunting, as are songbirds. The hunting lobby is a powerful force in politics. In a 1990 referendum it won the vote against a ban on hunting. On the positive side, laws are now in place to protect endangered species such as wolves, bears and boar. The setting up of reserves and national parks has helped to preserve some rare species. Italy has about 20 national parks, some of which date from the 1920s, and more are planned. Alpine parks such as Stelvio and Gran Paradiso protect chamois (a type of goat antelope), ibex (a type of wild goat) and marmots (ground squirrels), while mouflon sheep and boar roam in Sardinian reserves.

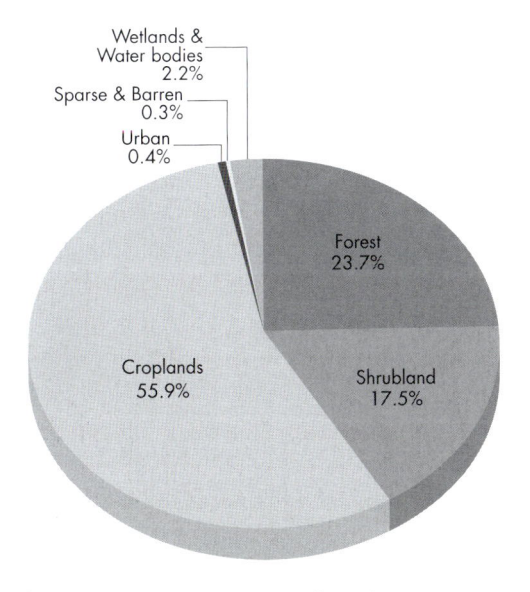

Environmental and conservation data

- Forested area as % total land area: 23.7
- Protected area as % total land area: 7.6
- Number of protected areas: 11,141

SPECIES DIVERSITY

Category	Known species	Threatened species
Mammals	269	45
Breeding birds	528	38
Reptiles	94	6
Amphibians	32	n/a
Fish	199	13
Plants	11,400	7

Source: World Resources Institute

Habitat type as percentage of total area:
- Forest 23.7%
- Shrubland 17.5%
- Croplands 55.9%
- Urban 0.4%
- Sparse & Barren 0.3%
- Wetlands & Water bodies 2.2%

Did you know?

Stelvio in the Alps of Lombardy is Italy's largest national park, covering 1,350 sq km (521 sq miles).

◀ Pony trekking offers an environmentally friendly way to see the landscape in Abruzzo National Park.

CHAPTER 14

Future Challenges

Italy entered the twenty-first century as a dynamic, prosperous nation with a well-developed economy. Italy's generous welfare system means that most of its people enjoy a good quality of life. However, persistent problems remain, including sluggish economic growth, organized crime and the divide between north and south.

DIVISIONS WITHIN ITALY

Despite the funds spent on the south since the 1950s, the country still divides into a prosperous north and a welfare dependent south with high unemployment. Much has been done to generate industry and improve the infrastructure in the south, but natural disadvantages remain. The government cannot change the harsh southern climate, which makes farming difficult, nor can it remedy the scarcity of resources. Future governments will need to try to continue supporting the south while placating the northern leagues – a difficult balancing act.

The political scandals of the 1990s caused a major shake-up in Italian politics but did little to reduce the country's bureaucracy, which stifles political and economic reform. Recent prime ministers have been elected on a pledge to root out organized crime and the Mafia. Yet the Mafia's octopus-like tentacles continue to reach all levels of Italian society.

▼ The wealth of the north is reflected in this affluent shopping centre in Milan.

Future Challenges 59

◀ Poverty is still a persistent problem in many parts of the south, including on the island of Sardinia. Poorer people, including members of ethnic minorities such as Roma (Gypsy) people, shown here, often struggle to survive.

WELFARE AND THE ECONOMY

Many analysts predict that Italy's population will fall within the next few decades. If current trends continue, the population may drop from 57 million to around 40 million by 2050. The growing numbers of older people will place an increasing burden on the state in terms of pensions, medical care and other benefits. The government recently reduced its financial commitments by changing the rules on pensions, including those of government employees. State employees used to be able to retire after 25 years' employment. This has been raised to 35 years, with a retirement age of 57. Meanwhile, to help pay for its welfare system, the government could gain additional contributions towards its Gross National Product if it were to succeed in levying taxes from those who operate within the informal or 'hidden' economy (see page 36).

Since the late 1950s, Italy has been at the forefront of European politics. Many Italians believe the European Union has had a positive effect on the country's economy, helping to tighten monetary policy and stimulate new growth. Many Italians look to the EU to lessen unemployment and keep inflation rates low. In recent decades, Italy has struggled with its balance of payments, with monies spent on imports exceeding the revenue from exports. Future governments will continue the effort to stimulate economic growth while considering the needs of the environment – another delicate balancing act.

Did you know?

Italy currently spends about 10 per cent of its Gross National Product on pensions – more than double the amount it spends on education.

Timeline

800-900 BC The Phoenicians colonize parts of southern Italy.
700-800 BC The Greeks found colonies in southern Italy.
600-700 BC The Etruscan civilization reaches its height in central Italy.
509 BC Etruscans are driven out of Rome by a Latin-speaking tribe, and Rome becomes a republic.
27 BC-AD 14 Augustus rules as the first Roman emperor.
AD 79 The eruption of Vesuvius destroys the Roman town of Pompeii.
117 The Roman Empire reaches its greatest extent, under the Emperor Trajan.
264 The start of the reign of Emperor Diocletian, during which the Roman Empire is divided into eastern and western halves.
330 Emperor Constantine moves capital of Roman Empire to Byzantium (now Istanbul).
476 Barbarian leader Odoacer sacks Rome and deposes the last western Roman emperor. The eastern branch, the Byzantine Empire, remains intact.
800 Land given to the pope by the Frankish king, Charlemagne, forms the basis of the Papal States. Charlemagne is crowned emperor of the Romans by the pope. This allegiance forms the basis for the Holy Roman Empire.
800-1100 Holy Roman emperors vie with successive popes for control of northern Italy. This rivalry allows for the emergence of the Italian city-states.
1000s The Normans colonize Sicily and southern Italy.
1265 The French become rulers of Sicily.
1300-1550 The age of the Renaissance.
c.1520-50 Spain and the Holy Roman Empire defeat France to control much of Italy.
1707 Austrian rulers take control of northern Italy.
1797 The French emperor, Napoleon Bonaparte, invades northern Italy, bringing the ideals of the French Revolution. He founds several republics.
1815 Napoleon is defeated, and Italy is returned to its former rulers, which include Austria and Spain.
1859-60 Piedmontese forces under Count Cavour defeat the Austrians in northern Italy and head south. Garibaldi and a force of 1,000 soldiers land in Sicily and move north to meet the Piedmontese army at Teano.
1861 The kingdom of Italy is proclaimed under the ruler of Piedmont-Sardinia, King Victor Emanuel II.
1866 Venice becomes part of the kingdom of Italy.
1870 The Papal States become part of Italy.
1908 A major earthquake strikes the port of Messina in Sicily, killing at least 70,000 people.
1911 Italy seizes Libya in North Africa.
1915-18 Italy sides with the Allies (Britain, France and Russia) during the First World War.
1922 Fascist leader Benito Mussolini becomes prime minister.
1925 Mussolini becomes dictator of all Italy.
1936 Italy seizes control of Ethiopia.
1940 Under Mussolini, Italy enters the Second World War on the side of Germany.
1945 War in Europe ends in victory for the Allies.
1946 Italy votes to abolish the monarchy and become a republic.
1948 Italy's new constitution comes into effect. Christian Democrats form the first of many coalition governments.
1950s Italy industrializes rapidly.
1950-1984 Italian governments fund the *Cassa per il Mezzogiorno* to develop the south.
1957 Italy becomes one of six nations to found the European Economic Community (EEC), which later becomes the European Union (EU).
1966 The River Arno floods in Florence, damaging art treasures. Venice also floods.
1970 Divorce is made legal in Italy.
1973-1980 The rise of terrorism in Italy by both right- and left-wing extremist groups.
1978 The Red Brigades kidnap and assassinate ex-prime minister Aldo Moro. Italians vote to make abortion legal. The election of a Polish cardinal as Pope John Paul II breaks with four hundred years of tradition, during which all popes have been Italian.
1980 An earthquake in Campania in southern Italy kills more than 4,500 people.
1983 Bettino Craxi becomes Italy's first socialist prime minister.
1985 Roman Catholicism is no longer Italy's state religion.
1987 A mass trial of Mafia suspects in Palermo results in 338 convictions.
1990 The political party called the Northern League emerges, calling for northern Italy to become independent of the south.
1992 Sicilian judge Giovanni Falcone is killed by a Mafia car bomb.
1992-3 The *Tangentopoli* political scandals bring about the downfall of many leading politicians and existing parties, such as the Christian Democrats. Birth of new political alliances.
1992 The EEC becomes the European Union (EU) with fifteen members.
1994 A coalition including *Forza Italia* led by Silvio Berlusconi takes power. However, Berlusconi resigns following accusations of corruption later the same year.
1994 Floods in north-west Italy kill more than one hundred people.
1996 The Olive Tree Alliance takes power in Italy.
2001 Silvio Berlusconi is re-elected prime minister.
2002 Italy adopts the single European currency.
2004 The EU expands to 25 members.
2005 Pope Benedict XVI became the 264th successor to St Peter.
September 2005 Italy seeks help from the EU to deal with the large numbers of illegal immigrants attempting to enter the country.
April 2006 A centre-left coalition led by Romano Prodi takes power after the narrowest of political victories.

Glossary

Allies The name given to the combined forces fighting against the German side during the First and Second World Wars. In the First World War, Britain, France, Italy and Russia and the USA fought against Germany, Austria-Hungary and Turkey. In the Second World War, Britain, France, the USA and the Soviet Union were allied against Germany, Italy and Japan.

Coalition A government formed by an alliance between several political parties.

Communist Party A political party advocating communism, a system of government in which power resides with a single party which controls all economic activity and provides services.

Conservative Having an outlook that opposes rapid change. In party politics, a right-wing party that supports private ownership.

Constitution A set of laws governing a country or organization.

Democracy A political system in which members of parliament are chosen by people voting in free elections.

Depose To overthrow.

Developed countries The richer countries of the world, whose industries are well-developed, including the USA, many European nations and Japan.

Dictator A ruler with absolute (complete) authority.

Erosion The wearing away of the land by natural forces, such as wind, rain and ice. Erosion is sometimes caused by deforestation.

Exodus A mass departure.

Fascist In politics, a party that favours strict government control of labour and industry. Power is often concentrated in the hands of a strong leader in fascist parties.

Fossil fuel Coal, oil, gas and other fuels formed from fossilized remains of plants or animals that lived millions of years ago.

Frankish Of or relating to the Franks, a Germanic nation that conquered France in the sixth century.

Fresco A mural painting in which the pigment (paint) is applied directly to wet plaster.

Geothermal energy Energy from hot rocks located underground.

Global warming Rising temperatures worldwide, caused by the increase of carbon dioxide and other gases in the atmosphere that trap the sun's heat.

Industrialization The process of developing a country's industries and manufacturing.

Inflation A general increase in prices within a country.

Infrastructure The facilities needed for a country to function, including communications and transport.

Internet host Internet site often representing an organization and ending in .com, .net or .org.

Irrigation The artificial watering of land in order to grow crops.

Liberal In general, tolerant or generous. Also describes political parties that support democratic reform and the abolition of privilege.

Literacy The ability to read and write.

North Atlantic Treaty Organization (NATO) A military alliance formed between the USA and several European countries following the Second World War. The aim of the alliance was to prevent a Soviet invasion of Europe.

Papacy The office of the pope, head of the Roman Catholic Church.

Papal Of, or belonging to, the pope.

Partisan A member of the Italian resistance during the Second World War, opposed to the Nazi Party and Mussolini.

Pollutant A substance that dirties the air, water or land when released.

Proportional representation A system of electing members of parliament by giving seats to political parties according to their share of the vote in the whole country.

Puppet state A state that is controlled by another, but with a nominal ruler who has little real power.

Quota A share allotted by agreement to a particular organization or country.

Reactor Part of a nuclear power plant where energy is made by splitting atoms.

Referendum A public vote on a single issue.

Republic A nation state without a monarch, ruled by the people or their representatives.

Risorgimento The movement to unify Italy in the 1800s; 'Resurrection' in Italian.

Sewage Dirty water from homes and factories, containing chemicals and human waste.

Tectonic plate One of the giant rigid sections that make up the earth's outer layer or crust.

Socialist Describes a person, or a political movement that favours a system of government in which a nation's wealth and infrastructure belong to all its citizens, not just to private individuals.

Subsidence When the ground level sinks.

Toll Fee charged for using a road or other transport link.

Turbine Machine powered by steam, gas or water that is used to generate electricity.

United Nations (UN) An organization founded at the end of the Second World War with the aim of preventing future wars. Today more than 150 nations belong to the UN.

Further Information

BOOKS TO READ

Countries of the World: Italy
Sally Garrington
(Evans Brothers, 2004)

Country Files: Italy
Ian Graham
(Franklin Watts, 2004)

Countrywise: Italy and Italian
Emma Sanstone
(Chrysalis Children's Books, 2003)

What's it Like to Live in: Italy?
Jillian Powell
(Hodder Wayland, 2003)

Rome (Alpha Holy Cities)
Nicola Barber
(Evans Brothers, 2003)

Heinemann Advanced History: Italian Unification 1820-71
Martin Collier
(Heinemann Educational, 2003)

Letter From Around the World: Italy
Fiona Tankard
(Cherrytree Books, 2002)

The Changing Face of: Italy
Kathryn Britton
(Hodder Wayland, 2002)

Living in: Italy
Ruth Thomson
(Franklin Watts, 2002)

FICTION

Escape from Pompeii
Christina Balit
(Henry Holt & Company, 2003)

The Name of the Rose (Vintage Classics)
Umberto Eco
(Vintage, paperback reissued 2004)

USEFUL WEBSITES

http://www.italyontheweb.org
Italy on the web, an official site providing information about Italy.

http://www.italiantouristboard.co.uk/
Italian State Tourist Board site for the UK.

www.cia.gov/cia/publications/factbook/geos/it.html
The CIA World Factbook, providing up-to-date statistics on Italy.

http://www.infoplease.com/ipa/A0107658.html
Information about Italy's geography, economy, government and people.

http://en.comuni-italiani.it/
Information and statistics on Italian regions, provinces and cities.

Index

Page numbers in **bold** indicate pictures.

Abruzzi 29
acid rain 54
air transport 40
Alliance for Freedom 24
Andreotti, Giulio 24, **24**
artists 46, **46**

Berlusconi, Silvio 24, 41
Bologna 43, **43**, 54
Bonaparte, Napoleon 10, 11
Borsellino, Paolo 25

Caboto, Giovanni 11
Calabria 26, 29, **49**
Capri 14, 53
Caselli, Giovanni 41
Cassa per il Mezzogiorno 20, 38
Cavour, Camillo 12
Christian Democrat Party 23, 24
Church, the 43, 48, 49, **49**
city-states 5, 6, 8, 10, 11, 20, 34
climate 16-17, 29, 50, 58
coal 26
Columbus, Christopher 11
communications 40, 41, **41**
Communist Party 23
culture 4, 5, 46, 47, 49, 50

deforestation 56
drugs trafficking 25, 36

earthquakes 15, 17
economy 4, 5, 13, 24, 30, 31, 35, 36, 53, 58, 59

education 42, **42**, 43, **43**, 44
Elba 14
electoral system 22
emigration 36-7
energy 26-7
environmental problems 54, 55, 56, 57, 59
Etna, Mount 15, 17
Etruscans 8
European Union (EU) 4, 34, 35, 59

Falcone, Giovanni 25, **25**
farming 17, 29, **29**, 32, 55
fashion industry 32, 33, **33**
festivals 49, **49**
FIAT 30
filmmaking 47
First World War 12
fishing 26, 28, 29
flooding 55, **55**, 56
Florence **5**, 20, 32, 52, 53, 54, 56
food 6, **6**, 44, **45**, 50, **50**, 51
forestry 26, 29
Forza Italia Party 24

Garibaldi, Giuseppe 12, **12**
gas 26
Genoa **11**, 20, 32, 39
geothermal energy 26
government 22-24, **23**
Greek Empire 8

healthcare 42, 44, **44**, 45
history 8-13
housing **18**, 21
hydro-electric power 26, **26**

immigration 37
industrialization 5, 13, 54
industry 26, 28, 30, 31, 32, 33, 34, **58**
inflation 24, 35, 59

lakes 15
language 6
Latini 8
Lega Lombardia 24
leisure activities 50, 51, 52
Liguria 56
literature 46
Lombardy 28, 29, 57

Mafia, the 6, 24, 25, **25**, 36, 58
manufacturing 30, 31, 32
marble 27, **27**, 28
Marconi, Guglielmo 41
Mazzini, Giuseppe 12
Mediterranean Sea 4, 14, 55
Michelangelo **5**, 27, 46
Milan 20, 24, 32, 33, **33**, 38, 39, 40, 47, 52, 54, **58**
minerals 26, 28, **28**
Moro, Aldo 13
mountains 14, **14**, 15, **52**
music 47, **47**
Mussolini, Benito 12, **13**, 22, 25, 39, 49

Naples 9, 20, **20**, 32, 39, **39**, 54
national parks 54, 57, **57**
newspapers 30, 41
North Atlantic Treaty Organization (NATO) 35
north-south divide 5, 31, 58
nuclear energy 26

oil 26, 34, 36
Olive Tree Alliance 24
organized crime *see* Mafia, the
overcrowding 21

papacy 5, 9, 48, 49
Papal States 10, 11, 12, 49
parliament 22, **22**
pasta 29, 44, 51
Pavarotti, Luciano 47
Piedmont 28, 56
Pliny the Younger 9
politics 5, 23, 24, 58
pollution 21, 53, 54, 55
Polo, Marco 11
Pompeii 9, **9**, 53
population 18-20, 59
Puglia 29, **29**

railways **38**, 39
recycling 56, **56**
Red Brigades 13

religion 9, 48
Renaissance 5, **5**, 10, 27, 46, 53
renewable energy 26
rivers 15, 40
roads 38, 39
Roman Empire 4, 8-9
Romans 4
Rome **4**, 5, **8**, 20, 40, 46, 48, **48**, 49, 52

San Marino 5
Sardinia 4, 6, 14, 17, 22, 28, 38, 39, **59**
Second World War 5, 12
service industries 31, **31**
shipyards **30**, 31
Sicily 4, **10**, 12, 14, 15, 17, 25, **25**, 26, 28, 29, 38, 53
sport 52

Tangentopoli scandals 23, 24, **24**
terrorism 13, 35
tourism 6, 31, **31**, 36, 52, **52**, 53
trade 34, 36
traffic congestion 21
transportation 38, **38**, 39, **39**, 40, **40**
Turin 30, 32, 52
Tuscany 27, 28

unemployment 20, 24, 30, 31, 58
unification 5, 11, 12
United Nations (UN) 35

Vatican City **4**, 5, 48, **48**
vegetation 17
Venice 10, 12, 20, 32, 40, **40**, 49, 52, 54, 55, **55**
Vespucci, Amerigo 11
Vesuvius, Mount 9, 15
Vinci, Leonardo da 46
volcanoes 15, **15**, 17

water transport 39, 40, **40**
wetlands 56
wildlife 54, 56, 57
women, role of 31, 45, 50
workforce 30, 31

About the Author

Dr Jen Green received a doctorate from the University of Sussex (Department of English and American Studies) in 1982. She worked in publishing for 15 years and is now a full-time writer who has written more than 150 books for children. She lives in Sussex.